50 WALKS

West Yorkshire

Published by AA Publishing (a trading name of AA Media Limited, whose registered office is Grove House, Lutyens Close, Lychpit, Basingstoke, Hampshire RG24 8AG; registered number 06112600)

© AA Media Limited 2013
First published 2001
Second edition 2009
Third edition 2013, reprinted 2014 (twice), 2015 (twice), 2016, 2017 (twice), 2018 and 2021

Researched and written by John Morrison
Field checked and updated 2013 by Dennis Kelsall

Mapping in this book is derived from the following products:
OS Landranger 103 (walks 32, 42, 46–49)
OS Landranger 104 (walks 6, 8, 9, 11–14, 16, 22–25, 27–30, 32–34, 36, 40, 45, 50)
OS Landranger 105 (walks 1, 3, 4, 6)
OS Landranger 109 (walk 41)
OS Landranger 110 (walks 18–21, 31, 35, 38, 39)
OS Landranger 111 (walks 5, 10, 15)
OS Explorer 21 (walks 43, 44)
OS Explorer 278 (walk 2)
OS Explorer 289 (walk 7)
OS Explorer 288 (walk 26)
OS Explorer 297 (walk 17)
© Crown copyright and database rights 2016 Ordnance Survey. 100021153.

ISBN: 978-0-7495-7488-8
ISBN (SS): 978-0-7495-7514-4

A CIP catalogue record for this book is available from the British Library.

Series management: David Popey
Editor: Sheila Hawkins Ltd
Designer: Tracey Freestone
Proofreader: Rebecca Needes
Digital imaging & repro: Ian Little
Cartography provided by the Mapping Services Department of AA Publishing

Printed and bound in the UK by Bell & Bain Ltd, Glasgow

A05792

The Automobile Association would like to thank the following photographers, companies and picture libraries for their assistance in the preparation of this book. Abbreviations for the picture credits are as follows: (t) top; (b) bottom; (l) left; (r) right; (AA) AA World Travel Library.
3 AA/J Tims; 9 AA/J Tims;
10 AA/J Tims; 12/13 AA/J Tims;
17 AA/J Morrison; 34/35 AA/J Tims;
52/53 AA/J Tims; 77 AA/P Wilson;
82 AA/D Clapp; 86/87 AA/T Mackie;
104/105 AA/J Tims; 135 AA/J Tims;
136 AA/P Wilson; 147 AA/J Tims;
158/159 AA/J Tims
Every effort has been made to trace the copyright holders, and we apologise in advance for any accidental errors. We would be happy to apply the corrections in the following edition of this publication.

Some of the walks may appear in other AA books and publications.

Discover and book AA-rated places to stay at RatedTrips.com

Right: Stoodley Pike on Pennine Way (Walk 42)

AA

50 WALKS IN
West Yorkshire

Contents

The walks

Following the walks

An information panel for each walk shows its relative difficulty, the distance and total amount of ascent. An indication of the gradients you will encounter is shown by the rating ▲▲▲ (no steep slopes) to ▲▲▲ (several very steep slopes). Each walk is rated for its relative difficulty compared to the other walks in this book. Walks marked +++ and colour-coded green are likely to be shorter and easier with little total ascent. Those marked with +++ and colour-coded orange are of intermediate difficulty. The hardest walks are marked +++ and are colour-coded red.

MAPS

There are 40 maps, covering the 50 walks. Some walks have a suggested option in the same area. The information panel for these walks will tell you how much extra walking is involved. On short-cut suggestions the panel will tell you the total distance if you set out from the start of the main walk. Where an option returns to the same point on the main walk, just the distance of the loop is given. Where an option leaves the main walk at one point and returns to it at another, then the distance shown is for the whole walk. The minimum time suggested is for reasonably fit walkers and doesn't allow for stops. Each walk has a suggested AA Walker's or Ornance Survey map.

ROUTE MAP LEGEND

_ _ _►_ _	Walk route	▦	Built-up area
1	Route waypoint	▦	Woodland area
_ _ _ _	Adjoining path	🚻	Toilet
⚜	Viewpoint	P	Car park
•	Place of interest	🪑	Picnic area
◠	Steep section	)(	Bridge

START POINTS

The start of each walk is given as a six-figure grid reference prefixed by two letters referring to a 100km square of the National Grid. You'll find more information on grid references on most Ordnance Survey and AA Walker's maps.

DOGS

We have tried to give dog owners useful advice about the dog friendliness of each walk. Please respect other countryside users. Keep your dog under control, especially around livestock, and obey local bylaws and other dog control notices.

CAR PARKING

Many of the car parks suggested are public, but occasionally you may find you have to park on the roadside or in a lay-by. Please be considerate when you leave your car, ensuring that access roads or gates are not blocked and that other vehicles can pass safely.

WALKS LOCATOR

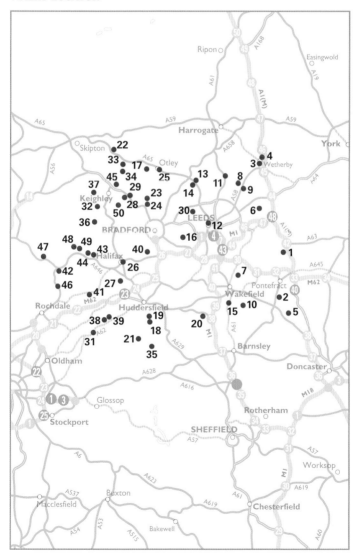

Walking in West Yorkshire

Everybody knows that Yorkshire has some special landscapes. Out in the Dales, the Moors, the Wolds and the Pennine hills, walkers can lengthen their stride, breathe fresh country air and be alone with their thoughts. But what about West Yorkshire? That's Leeds and Bradford isn't it? Back-to-back houses, blackened mills, chip shops... There's more than a little truth to most clichés. Hebden Bridge is a case in point. If you had stood on any of the surrounding hills a hundred years ago, and gazed down into the valley, all you would have seen was the pall of smoke issuing from the chimneys of 33 textile mills. The town itself would have appeared just once each year: during the Wakes Week holiday, when the mills were shut.

GOOD WALKING

Thankfully, life changes and here in West Yorkshire, it can change very quickly indeed. The textile trade went into terminal decline. The mills shut down forever. In a single generation Hebden Bridge changed from being a place that people wanted to leave, to a place that people want to visit. The countryside around Hebden Bridge offers walking every bit as good as the more celebrated Yorkshire Dales; within minutes, you can be tramping across the moors. And this close proximity of town and country is repeated all across West Yorkshire.

EAST AND WEST

You may notice that the west of the county is favoured a little more strongly than the east. To the west, where the Pennine hills create a natural barrier between the old foes of Yorkshire and Lancashire, is a truly wild landscape. This is where Pennine Way-farers get into their stride. Here are heather moors, riven by steep-sided wooded valleys known as 'cloughs'. Here are empty acres, sheep-cropped grass and the evocative cry of the curlew.

WIDE OPEN SPACES

Local folk have a great fondness for the landscapes of West Yorkshire, and for a good reason. The expansion of industry – particularly the textile trades – forced a great many people off the land and into the towns. For generations the open spaces represented fresh air and freedom for those who laboured six days a week at the textile mills of Leeds, Bradford, Huddersfield, Batley and the other centres of industry along the valleys of the Rivers Colne, Aire and Calder. For those who value solitude, and wide open spaces, try walks 31, 32, 34, 37, 41 and 42.

Right: View over Lower Laithe Reservoir from the Pennine Way near Stanbury (Walk 32)

WILD OASES

The Pennine moors are rightly valued for their wild beauty. But we should also cherish the rural oases nearer to the West Yorkshire towns. Walks such as 5, 12, 15, 40 and 50 are valuable precisely because they are so close to centres of population. You will find beautiful deciduous woodlands, country parks, and the wildlife 'corridors' provided by canal tow paths and old railway lines.

Lovers of wildlife have a wide choice of walks. The Pennine moors are home to birds such as red grouse, kestrels and ring ouzels; the fast-flowing rivers support dippers and wagtails. To see rare birds you should head to the east of the county where opencast coal mines have been reinvented as lakes and wetlands. Walks 1, 5, 7 and 10 visit some of the most interesting sites.

A WEALTH OF CHOICE

There's such diversity in the area that you can find yourself in quite unfamiliar surroundings, even close to places you may know very well. Take time to explore this rich county on foot and you will be thrilled at what you find to shatter old myths and preconceptions.

PUBLIC TRANSPORT West Yorkshire has an enviable public transport system. Most of these walks are within easy reach of frequent and relatively cheap buses and trains. For timetable information call Metroline on 0113 245 7676, or visit www.wymetro.com. You can also find bus and train information at www.traveline.info.

Above: Breary Marsh (Walk 13)

Walking in safety

All these walks are suitable for any reasonably fit person, but less experienced walkers should try the easier walks first. Route finding is usually straightforward, but you will find that an AA walking map or an Ordnance Survey map is a useful addition to the route maps and descriptions; recommendations can be found in the information panels.

RISKS

Although each walk here has been researched with a view to minimising the risks to the walkers who follow its route, no walk in the countryside can be considered to be completely free from risk. Walking in the outdoors will always require a degree of common sense and judgement to ensure that it is as safe as possible.

- Be aware of the consequences of changes in the weather and check the forecast before you set out. Carry spare clothing and a torch if you are walking in the winter months. Remember the weather can change very quickly at any time of the year, and in moorland and heathland areas, mist and fog can make route finding much harder. Don't set out in these conditions unless you are confident of your navigation skills in poor visibility. In summer remember to take account of the heat and sun; wear a hat and carry water.
- Be particularly careful on cliff paths and in upland terrain, where the consequences of a slip can be very serious.
- Remember to check tidal conditions before walking on the seashore.
- Some sections of route are by, or cross, busy roads. Take care and remember traffic is a danger even on minor country lanes.
- Be careful around farmyard machinery and livestock, especially if you have children with you.
- On walks away from centres of population you should carry a whistle and survival bag. If you do have an accident requiring the emergency services, make a note of your position as accurately as possible and dial 999.

COUNTRYSIDE CODE

- Be safe, plan ahead and follow any signs.
- Leave gates and property as you find them.
- Protect plants and animals and take your litter home.
- Keep dogs under close control.
- Consider other people.

For more information visit:
www.gov.uk/government/publications/the-countryside-code

Overleaf: Golden Acre Park (Walk 13)

Fairburn Ings and Ledsham

DISTANCE 5 miles (8km)   MINIMUM TIME 1hrs 45min

ASCENT/GRADIENT 262ft (80m) ▲▲▲   LEVEL OF DIFFICULTY ✦✦✦

PATHS Good paths and tracks

LANDSCAPE Lakes, riverside and reclaimed colliery spoil heaps

SUGGESTED MAP OS Explorer 289 Leeds

START/FINISH Grid reference: SE470278

DOG FRIENDLINESS Keep on lead around main lake, due to wildfowl

PARKING Free parking in Cut Road, Fairburn, 100yds (91m) west of the Three Horseshoes pub, in the direction of Fairburn Ings

PUBLIC TOILETS Fairburn Ings Visitor Centre

The coalfields of West Yorkshire were most concentrated in the borough of Wakefield. Towns and villages grew up around the mines, and came to represent the epitome of northern industrial life. Mining was always a dangerous and dirty occupation, and it changed the landscape dramatically. Opencast mines swallowed up huge tracts of land, and the extensive spoil heaps were all-too-visible evidence of industry.

For the men of these communities, mining was almost the only work available. So when the industry went into decline, these communities were hit especially hard. The mining industry was decimated and thousands of miners lost their livelihoods.

The death of the industry was emphasised by the closing down of Caphouse Colliery and its subsequent conversion into the National Coal Mining Museum for England. However, the spoil heaps that once scarred the landscape are going back to nature, a process hastened by tree planting and other reclamation schemes. Opencast workings have been transformed into lakes and wetlands – valuable havens for wildfowl and migrating birds – and West and South Yorkshire has achieved a network of lakes to rival the Norfolk Broads.

FAIRBURN INGS NATURE RESERVE

Fairburn Ings, now under the stewardship of the Royal Society for the Protection of Birds (RSPB), was one of the earliest examples of colliery reclamation – being designated a Local Nature Reserve in 1957. The stark outlines of the spoil heaps are now softened by banks of silver birch, and mining subsidence has created a broad expanse of water near the village of Fairburn, as well as smaller pools and flashes.

There are plenty of birds to be seen at all times of the year, though the numbers of ducks, geese, swans and gulls are at their highest during the winter months. The 600 acres (243ha) of wetlands are a magnet for birds during the spring and autumn migration. In summer there are many species of wildlife nesting on the scrapes and islands – including terns and a large, noisy colony of black-headed gulls. The best places from which to view all this activity are the public hides that overlook the lake.

LEDSHAM

Hidden away from the nearby motorway traffic, Ledsham is a tranquil little backwater. Behind its Saxon church – one of the oldest in West Yorkshire – is a row of picturesque almshouses. The village has an old and characterful country pub, the Chequers Inn.

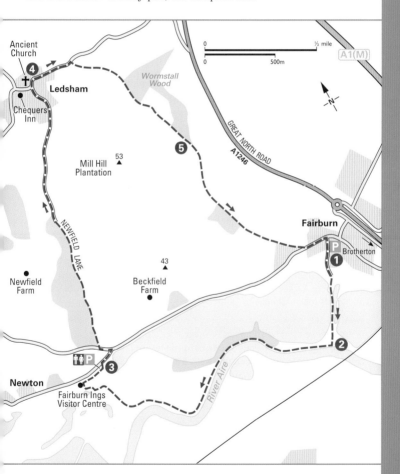

❶ Walk down Cut Road. After passing through a gate, the way narrows to a wooded causeway between the lakes, from which a

short detour leads to a bird hide over on the left. The route, however, remains with the main path, crossing a bridge and eventually leading to a junction overlooking the River Aire.

2 Go right through a kissing gate along the top of a wooded ridge (actually an old spoil heap), which separates the river from the lake. Look out for a couple of other bird hides before you lose sight of the lake. As the ridge broadens, the path diverges from the river. Later falling, it curves to join a track above a smaller lake. Follow it down right to a metal gate and go left in front of it through a kissing gate. After 100yds (91m), opposite a sculpted frog, turn right on a walkway that winds across a marsh to the visitor centre. Swing right through the car park to a lane.

3 Go right to a junction and turn left towards Ledston and Kippax. However, after just 100yds (91m), take a path on your right that hugs the right-hand fringe of a wood. Beyond the trees, the way continues between fields, broadening to a track as it nears Ledsham. Emerging onto Manor

Garth, go right to the main lane in front of the church.

4 The Chequers Inn lies a short distance to the left. The return route, however, winds to the right around the church and through the village. After 200yds (183m), on a left bend, leave ahead through a gate onto an undulating track. Go over a stile, walk towards woodland and continue within its periphery. Beyond another stile, keep going beside the trees and then on again at the bottom of a pasture. A stile left of the corner takes the way through a narrow spur of woodland.

5 Head slightly left, uphill, across the next field, to follow a fence and hedgerow bounding the top. Keep ahead through kissing gates, remaining at the field-edge and passing barns that stand over to the left. Through a final gate, a developing track leads downhill. Go left when you eventually meet the road, back into the village of Fairburn.

WHERE TO EAT AND DRINK Chequers Inn in Ledsham harks back to the past in more ways than one. The exposed beams and open fires give the pub a homely atmosphere. Excellent food makes the place popular for lunches with walkers and locals (open Monday to Saturday 11–11, Sunday 12–6).

WHAT TO SEE Be sure to take a pair of binoculars with you. Fairburn Ings is a bird reserve of national importance and, especially during the spring and autumn migrations, all kinds of rare birds can be seen. There are a number of strategically sited hides along this walk, from which you can watch the birds without disturbing them. Watch especially for the rare but inconspicuous gadwall, pochard and golden plover.

WHILE YOU'RE THERE Old and new coexist at Ferrybridge, gateway to West Yorkshire from the south and east. A sprawling interchange joins the M62 and A1(M) beside the huge cooling towers of the Ferrybridge Power Station, but nearby, alongside the modern span carrying the A162 (formerly A1) across the River Aire is a surprising anachronism: an 18th-century bridge by the Yorkshire architect John Carr, better known for his work on Harewood House.

Right: Fairburn Ings (Walk 1)

High Ackworth and East Hardwick

DISTANCE 5.5 miles (8.8km)   MINIMUM TIME 2hrs

ASCENT/GRADIENT 180ft (55m) ▲▲▲   LEVEL OF DIFFICULTY ✦✦✦

PATHS Mostly field paths, several stiles

LANDSCAPE Gently rolling, arable country

SUGGESTED MAP OS Explorer 278 Sheffield & Barnsley

START/FINISH Grid reference: SE440180

DOG FRIENDLINESS Dogs on leads in villages and through farmyards

PARKING A few parking places in middle of High Ackworth, near church and village green

PUBLIC TOILETS None on route

High Ackworth has a pleasantly old-fashioned air and is now designated a conservation area. Today the village is best known for its school, founded by a prominent Quaker, John Fothergill. Ackworth Quaker School opened its doors on 18 October, 1779, a day still commemorated by the pupils as Founder's Day. Opposite the village green are almshouses, built in 1741 to house 'a schoolmaster and six poor women'.

Nearby Ackworth Old Hall, dating from the early 17th century, is supposed to be haunted by John Nevison, a notorious robber and highwayman. His most famous act of daring was in 1676 when he rode from Rochester to York in just 15 hours. The story goes that he committed a robbery and then was afraid his victim might have recognised him. Fleeing the scene, he put the 230 miles (373km) behind him in record time. On his arrival in York, Nevison was seen asking the Lord Mayor the time. After his arrest he used the Mayor as his alibi and was acquitted. This amazing feat of horsemanship is often wrongly attributed to another highwayman, Dick Turpin, who was not yet born.

PLAGUE STORY

Until the Reformation, the stone plinth on the village green was topped by a cross. The cross had been erected in memory of Father Thomas Balne of nearby Nostell Priory, who once preached from here. During a pilgrimage to Rome, he succumbed to the plague. When his body was being brought back to the priory, mourners insisted on opening the coffin here in High Ackworth. As a result, the plague was inflicted upon the community, with devastating results. The Plague Stone, by the Pontefract Road, dates from a second devastating outbreak in 1645 (see While You're There).

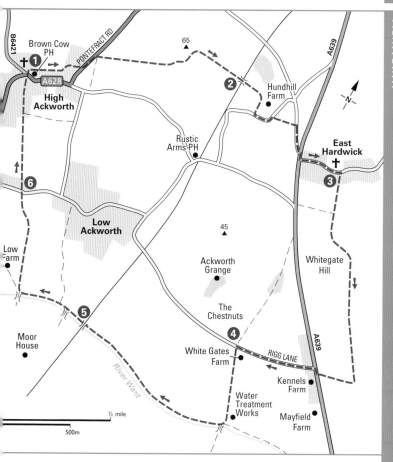

❶ From the top of the village green, take a narrow ginnel immediately to the right of Manor House. Beyond a stile made of stone slabs (not the last you'll see today), keep by the right-hand edge of a field to another stile. Another passage leads out into Woodland Grove; walk left then first right to meet the A628, Pontefract Road. Go left for just 100yds (91m), crossing to a signed gap in the hedgerow (opposite a house called Tall Trees). Guided by the left-most finger, head across to a tiny footbridge over a beck at the far side. Continue along the right-hand edge of the next two fields. In the third, dogleg left and right to continue beside the

hedge, which then curves left. After some 150yds (137m) watch for a waymarked trod striking right, due east across the open field. Continue across a second field to a bridge spanning a railway.

❷ Maintain your direction between fields towards Hundhill Farm. By the farm, turn within the field corner along its bottom edge to a stile. Emerging on to a lane, go left, walking 100yds (91m) to round a bend. Immediately after, go over a stile on the right to follow an enclosed path. Beyond the next stile, turn right along a minor road that soon meets the A639. Cross to Darrington Road opposite, passing the old village pump, and walk into East Hardwick. Where the road swings left, look for a bridleway sign on your right, just before a house called Bridleways.

3 The track leads away between the fields behind, shortly bending sharply left. Carry on for a further 100yds then swing off into a narrow field on the right. Accompany the right-hand hedge to the top of the strip, there dog-legging right and left to continue between open fields. Meeting a crossing track at the end, go right to come out on the main road by a junction. Cross and follow Rigg Lane opposite for some 650yds (0.6km) to White Gates Farm, where a concrete bridletrack on the left is signed to Burnhill Bridge.

4 Follow this track past a water treatment works, to a concrete bridge over the River Went (notice the old packhorse bridge next to it). Without crossing either bridge, turn right, on a field-edge path, to accompany the river. A little plank bridge takes you across a side-beck. Now walk beneath a six-arched railway viaduct.

5 Ignoring a field access bridge, continue to a waymarked junction just a little beyond. Bear left through a hedge gap and over a bridged ditch to remain with the main river. Reaching a stone bridge near Low Farm, swing right to a gate beside barns. Walk on at the edge of a large crop field and then a playing field to emerge in Low Ackworth.

6 Diagonally cross the road to a path between houses. Beyond a stile at the far end, bear half left across a field. Keep going across another field towards more houses, emerging over a stile between them. Walk forward along Hill Drive and then turn right down a cul-de-sac. At the bottom, take another passage on the left to arrive back in High Ackworth near the village green.

WHERE TO EAT AND DRINK The Brown Cow at the walk's start serves evening meals from Tuesday to Saturday and lunches on Sunday. Otherwise, try the nearby Rustic Arms on Long Lane in Low Ackworth. It serves food daily from noon and is set within its own grounds overlooking a lake.

WHAT TO SEE Village greens are uncommon features in West Yorkshire, a county in which even the smallest community can feel like a town. But the Industrial Revolution passed Ackworth by; no mill chimneys ever disturbed the symmetry. Surrounded by buildings of character – including the parish church, Manor House and a row of almshouses – Ackworth has managed to retain its village atmosphere.

WHILE YOU'RE THERE The Plague Stone stands outside Ackworth, at the junction of the A628 Pontefract Road and Sandy Gate Lane. It is an evocative relic of when the Black Death swept through these communities, in 1645, killing over 150 villagers. The hollow in the stone would have been filled with vinegar to disinfect coins left in payment for food brought from outside the village while it was in quarantine. The victims are thought to have been buried in the 'Burial Field' a few hundred paces to the east. The year before the same fields had witnessed bloody skirmishing between the Parliamentarian troops and Royalists, and may have already been used for mass burials.

Wetherby and the River Wharfe

DISTANCE 4 miles (6.4km)   MINIMUM TIME 1hr 30min

ASCENT/GRADIENT 164ft (50m) ▲▲▲   LEVEL OF DIFFICULTY ✚✚✚

PATHS Field paths and good tracks, a little road-walking, no stiles

LANDSCAPE Arable land, mostly on the flat

SUGGESTED MAP OS Explorer OL289 Leeds

START/FINISH Grid reference: SE404480

DOG FRIENDLINESS Keep on lead along roads and by racecourse

PARKING Free car parking in Wilderness car park, on right immediately over bridge when approaching Wetherby from the south

PUBLIC TOILETS Wetherby

Wetherby, at the northeast corner of the county, is not your typical West Yorkshire town. Most of the houses are built of pale stone, topped with red-tiled roofs – a type of architecture more usually found in North Yorkshire. With its riverside developments and air of prosperity, the Wetherby of today is a favoured place to live. The flat, arable landscape, too, is different to Pennine Yorkshire. Here, on the fringes of the Vale of York, the soil is rich and dark and productive – the fields divided up by fences and hedgerows rather than dry-stone walls.

HISTORIC TOWN

A glance at an Ordnance Survey map reveals that Wetherby grew up around a tight curve in the River Wharfe. Its importance as a river crossing was recognised by the building of a castle, possibly in the 12th century, of which only the foundations remain. The first mention of a bridge was in 1233. A few years later, in 1240, the Knights Templar were granted a royal charter to hold a market in Wetherby.

At Flint Mill, passed on this walk, flints were ground for use in the pottery industry of Leeds, and there were also two corn mills, powered by water from the River Wharfe. In general though, the Industrial Revolution made very little impression on Wetherby.

The town grew in importance not from what it made, but from where it was situated – at the halfway point of a journey between London and Edinburgh. Wetherby became a convenient stop for mail and passenger coaches and inns, such as the Swan & Talbot and the Angel (now an Italian restaurant) catered to weary travellers and provided stabling for the horses. The Great North Road ran across the town's splendid arched bridge, and right through the middle of the town. With coaches arriving and departing daily, it must have presented a busy scene.

When the railway arrived in the 1840s, Wetherby's role as a staging post went into decline. The Great North Road was eventually re-routed around the town, known simply as the A1, until it was upgraded to motorway status as the A1(M). When Dr Beeching wielded his axe in 1964, Wetherby lost its railway too. Ironically, a town that was once synonymous with coach travel is now a peaceful backwater and upmarket commuter town. The area around the River Wharfe has been renovated to provide apartments, pleasant walks and picnic sites.

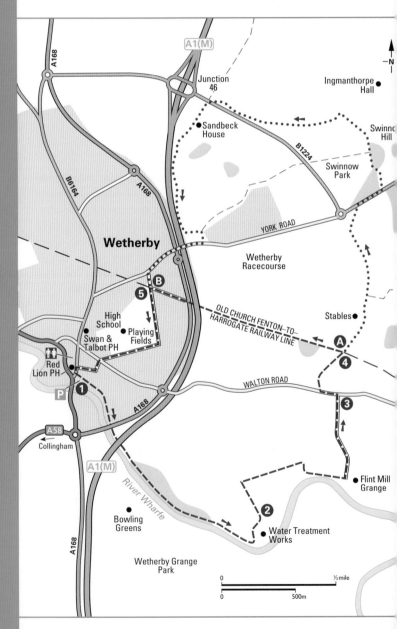

① Walk to the far end of the car park, to follow a path at the foot of low cliffs beside the River Wharfe. You pass in quick succession beneath the shallow spans of three modern bridges, carrying the A168 and A1(M) roads across the Wharfe. Emerging beyond, walk the length of a narrow pasture, passing through a kissing gate at the far end by Wetherby's Water Treatment Works.

② Turn left beside the perimeter fence to the plant entrance and go left again along a metalled drive. After 300yds (274m), meeting a junction of tracks at the top of a rise, turn off right along a field track. Carry on along the top of a wooded bank that falls to the River Wharfe, emerging onto the bend of another drive at Flint Mill Grange. Go left and walk out to the main road.

③ Turn left along Walton Road. After 75yds (69m) cross to a gated drive on the right, an entrance to Wetherby Racecourse and a bridleway through to York Road. Walk for 0.25 miles (400m), to meet a crossing track, Point ⓐ. The longer walk continues along the drive ahead.

④ To return directly to Wetherby, however, turn left, dropping onto the trackbed of the old Church Fenton-to-Harrogate railway line, which carried its last train in 1964. A mile's (1.6km) easy walking takes you to the A1(M) motorway, raised up on an embankment as it skirts around Wetherby. Take the underpass beneath the road, and keep ahead along Freemans Way, until you meet Hallfield Lane.

⑤ Walk left, along Hallfield Lane, following it right around the playing fields of Wetherby High School towards the town centre. At the end, bear left into Nags Lane, right along Victoria Street and then go left back to the river.

WHERE TO EAT AND DRINK As a market town, and a staging post on the Great North Road, Wetherby is well provided with a choice of pubs, cafes and old coaching inns. The Red Lion on the High Street near the start of the walk serves traditional bar meals at very reasonable prices. It's open every day, as is the Swan & Talbot, higher up into the town on North Street, which prides itself on great food.

WHAT TO SEE Unlike many towns in West Yorkshire, Wetherby still holds its general market every Thursday, with the stalls arranged around the handsome little town hall. Nearby are the Shambles, a row of colonnaded stalls built in 1811 to house a dozen butchers' shops.

WHILE YOU'RE THERE Wetherby's nearest neighbour is Boston Spa which, like Ilkley, became a prosperous spa town on the River Wharfe. It was the accidental discovery, in 1744, of a mineral spring that changed the town's fortunes. The salty taste and sulphurous smell were enough to convince people that the spring water had health-giving properties, and a pump room and bath house were built to cater to well-heeled visitors. The town's great days as a spa town are over but, with some splendid Georgian buildings, it has retained an air of elegance.

Wetherby Racecourse

DISTANCE 6 miles (9.7km)   MINIMUM TIME 2hrs 30min

ASCENT/GRADIENT 197ft (60m) ▲▲▲   LEVEL OF DIFFICULTY ✚✚✚

SEE MAP AND INFORMATION PANEL FOR WALK 3

The flat landscape around Wetherby lent itself to arable and dairy farming, while horse racing was a popular pursuit on nearby Clifford Moor by the 17th century. But racing didn't find a permanent home at Wetherby until 1891, when a course was laid out on land belonging to the Montagu family of nearby Ingmanthorpe Hall. In 1929 a railway station was built alongside the racecourse.

Of the nine racecourses in Yorkshire, Wetherby is the only one devoted entirely to racing over jumps, attracting the best steeplechasers from all over the country. It stages top quality National Hunt race days between October and May, as well as a perennially popular two-day meeting at Christmas.

At Point **Ⓐ**, continue along the metalled drive, which shortly leads to the Wetherby racecourse. Keep ahead with the main drive past the stabling areas and car parks and then the race track itself. Approaching the vehicle exit, bear off right across the last car park to find a small gate in the boundary hedge – it's hidden just beyond a clump of scrub. Go right, along the road, for 200yds (183m),

then bear left along a metalled drive signed to Swinnow Hill. After 200yds (183m), look for a double gate on the left. Through that, turn right on a waymarked bridleway around the perimeter of a wood, continuing between the fields beyond its end to meet Sandbeck Lane opposite the entrance to the imposing Ingmanthorpe Hall.

Turn left along the lane until you reach a bend. There keep straight ahead past a gate along a hedged farm track. The track meanders pleasantly between large fields of rich brown soil before turning out to meet the B1224 near its roundabout junction with the motorway and service area. Turn right, crossing to a track that leads away past buildings and then runs for a short distance along an embankment above the motorway. Eventually, it swings away to a junction, where you should go right to emerge on to another road. Follow it over the motorway bridge into the outskirts of the town and carry on for a further 300yds (274m), before turning left into Hallfield Lane, rejoining Walk 3 a short distance along at Point **Ⓑ**.

Upton's reclaimed country

DISTANCE 3.5 miles (5.7km)	MINIMUM TIME 1hr 15min

ASCENT/GRADIENT 197ft (60m) ▲▲▲   LEVEL OF DIFFICULTY ✚✚✚

PATHS Disused railway line and good tracks

LANDSCAPE Reclaimed colliery land

SUGGESTED MAP OS Explorer 278 Sheffield & Barnsley

START/FINISH Grid reference: SE478132

DOG FRIENDLINESS Keep on lead near roads

PARKING Car park off Waggon Lane, Upton, next to fishing lake

PUBLIC TOILETS None on route

The scenery of the southeastern corner of West Yorkshire contrasts markedly with the high moorlands to the west. Breaking from the hills, the rivers twist across a flatter landscape more suited to agriculture than the abrupt slopes and bleak tops of the Pennines. Further west, the towns had grown out of narrow valleys, where fast-flowing streams had powered the beginnings of the Industrial Revolution, but here, it was what lay below the ground that would make the difference.

YORKSHIRE'S GOLD

Although Yorkshire's coal has probably been dug since Roman times, it was not until the end of the 18th century that mining was developed on any significant scale. Lack of practical transportation and technical knowledge had limited activity to readily accessible outcrops that were worked from shallow bell pits or drifts. The change came with the development of river navigations, canals and subsequent railways, and towns and villages sprang up around the pitheads housing close-knit communities that depended upon the mines for their livelihood.

The burgeoning steam age brought an almost insatiable demand for coal and in the early 20th century, mines were sunk ever deeper. The area became one of the largest coal producers in the country, but things were already changing; foreign competition and a gradual drift to oil as a primary fuel heralded a contracting market. Changes brought in by Nationalisation after World War II were not enough to save the mines and wholesale closures from the mid-1980s finished the industry.

A NEW LIFE

The mines of the industrial age changed the landscape irrevocably, in places creating barren moonscapes of mountainous tips and vast craters. Equally dramatic are the changes of the last 30 years. Great heaps of spoil have been graded and planted with grasses, shrubs and trees, water has flooded opencast workings to create lakes, while disued railway lines now serve as footpaths and cycle routes.

The first half of this walk follows the course of the now closed Hull and Barnsley Railway. Along the way are the remains of Upton Station, embankments and cuttings, and at the halfway point is Johnny Brown's Common, a former tip at the foot of which is a large lake.

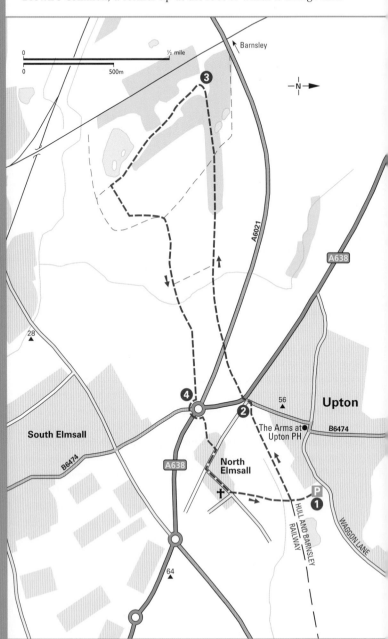

1 Leave the Upton Recreation Area car park through a kissing gate by a fishing pond. Turn right to a second kissing gate and follow the cinder track bed of the former Hull and Barnsley Railway to the right. Keep to the main path, passing a tree-fringed pond, and then later pass the overgrown platform of Upton and North Elmsall Station. Finally, emerge through a gate beside a junction of roads with the A638.

2 Carefully cross the main road to pick up the ongoing track opposite. Signed as a bridleway, it runs within a wooded cutting to a second main road (A6021). Again, cross the road and continue to walk along the former railway line, which alternates between embankment and cutting across the far-reaching, rolling countryside. The path eventually rises onto more open ground, then shortly meets a broad trail near the crest of the hill.

3 Turning sharp left, descend between the trees towards a lake that soon appears ahead. Bear left at a fork to pass around the eastern bank. Meeting a crossing track at its far end, go left. Keep with it as it subsequently swings left and then right. Continue for another 0.75 miles (1.2km) before ultimately coming out at a large roundabout.

4 Following bridleway signs anticlockwise around the roundabout, cross the B6474 and then the A638 before turning off down a truncated minor road into North Elmsall. At the end go right and then left into Hall Lane. Walk up to a junction just beyond the church. There, leave over a stone stile on the left. A sign to Upton points a diagonal line across a couple of fields. At the far side, cross a drainage ditch and walk forward to a final stile. Rejoining the course of the railway, go right and then left back to the car park.

WHERE TO EAT AND DRINK The Arms at Upton, on Upton High Street, is conveniently placed near the start of this walk for refreshments.

WHAT TO SEE The first part of this walk uses a section of the old Hull and Barnsley Railway. The trains are long gone; this narrow corridor, between the fields that stretch away on either side, is now a haven for wildlife. Judicious planting has created an excellent habitat for butterflies; look out for such colourful summer sights as the orange tip, the peacock, the painted lady and the red admiral.

WHILE YOU'RE THERE Close by is Cusworth Hall, a splendid mid-18th-century mansion, which houses permanent displays revealing the area's social history as well as a varied programme of occasional exhibits and events. The extensive grounds are managed as a country park and support a wealth of wildlife including Daubenton's bat, which flies low over the lakes at dusk feeding on insects.

Barwick in Elmet

DISTANCE 10 miles (16.1km)	MINIMUM TIME 3hrs 30min
ASCENT/GRADIENT 508ft (155m) ▲▲▲	LEVEL OF DIFFICULTY ✚✚✚
PATHS Field paths; good track through Parlington Estate	
LANDSCAPE Arable, parkland, woods	
SUGGESTED MAP OS Explorer 289 Leeds	
START/FINISH Grid reference: SE399374	
DOG FRIENDLINESS Keep on lead through villages and past golf course	
PARKING Roadside parking in Barwick in Elmet, near maypole	
PUBLIC TOILETS None on route	

Elmet was one of a number of small, independent British kingdoms to emerge during the so-called Dark Ages, between the end of Roman rule and the conquering of southern Britain, in AD 560, by the Saxon King Edwin. At the height of its powers the kingdom included most of present-day West Yorkshire, and extended from the River Humber in the east, to the Pennine hills in the west. Whilst it is known that Elmet was a realm of some importance, there is little solid archaeological evidence for its existence, apart from a series of defensive earthworks.

BARWICK IN ELMET

This is one of West Yorkshire's most ancient settlements. Before the Roman invasion it was a town of some size, and after the Romans had left the area it became the capital of the local kingdom of Elmet. A road, 'The Boyle', bends around the castle mound: here was a 12th-century Norman fortification, built on the site of an Iron Age hill-fort. The town also boasts the second tallest maypole in the country.

ABERFORD

The road that runs through Aberford is of Roman origin, built around AD 70. On an Ordnance Survey map you can trace its orientation from Aberford down to Castleford – look for Roman Ridge Road. Aberford was once an important stopping point on the Great North Road, where its roadside coaching inns provided shelter for both horses and riders.

Black Horse Farm, to the north of the town, was once the Black Horse Inn, a favourite haunt of John Nevison, a famous local highwayman. When he rode from London to York in a single day, he changed horses at the Black Horse. The great road of today, better known as the A1(M), makes the smallest of detours, around the town, to allow the juggernauts to hurry past at speed. This leaves Aberford pleasantly quiet and free from the roar of traffic.

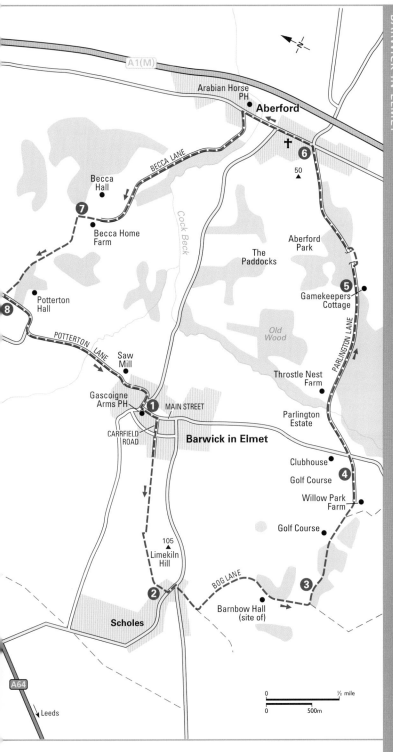

Arabian Horse PH
Aberford
Becca Hall
Becca Home Farm
Potterton Hall
Becca Lane
Cock Beck
The Paddocks
Aberford Park
Gamekeepers Cottage
Parlington Lane
Old Wood
Potterton Lane
Saw Mill
Gascoigne Arms PH
Main Street
Carrfield Road
Barwick in Elmet
Throstle Nest Farm
Parlington Estate
Clubhouse
Golf Course
Willow Park Farm
Golf Course
Limekiln Hill
Bog Lane
Barnbow Hall (site of)
Scholes
A64
Leeds

A1(M)

0   ½ mile
0   500m

❶ Walk south along Main Street from the maypole past the store and post office. After 250yds (229m) turn right into Carrfield Road. Beyond the end, keep ahead along a grass track and then a field path. Entering the third field swing right to pass through a gap in the corner and then left beside the hedge. Cross back through further on, eventually coming out onto a lane at Scholes.

❷ Go left for 100yds (91m) to a road off right, signed to Leeds. Cross to a stony bridleway beside the intersection, soon leaving Scholes behind. At a junction, keep left on the most obvious track. When another track comes in from the left, keep ahead past a barrier. Walk a further 0.5 miles (800m) to a junction. There, go left with the bridleway beside a small wood.

❸ Passing onto a golf course, walk forward along the main path, ignoring two footpaths subsequently signed off on the right. Leave the far end of the course along a track that soon passes Willow Park Farm. Keep straight ahead to meet a road near the golfers' clubhouse.

❹ Cross the road and continue on a farm track into the Parlington Estate. Carry on for 0.75 miles (1.2km) beyond Throstle Nest Farm to a junction beside Gamekeepers Cottage, a curious-looking house with a wall around it.

❺ Keep straight ahead along the bridleway through woodland. Bear right, just before a tunnel, to avoid walking through the gloom. The path rejoins your original route at the far end of the tunnel. Pass a gatehouse to arrive in the village of Aberford.

❻ Walk left, along the road, crossing a bridge over Cock Beck and then passing a pub named the Arabian Horse. Go left, opposite this pub, along Becca Lane. Keep left when it forks past Cufforth House and continue beyond a gatehouse into the parkland surrounding Becca Hall. After another 0.25 miles (400m), look for a waymark signing the path off left at the edge of the pasture. Later developing as a track, it leads to Becca Farm.

❼ Continue ahead on the farm track but, just after the barns, turn left at a discrete waymarker post and strike out over the field to a second marker post. Beyond a solitary tree, swing right towards the corner of woodland ahead and follow the ongoing boundary to another belt of trees. Over a stile, bear left to emerge in the next field and keep left along its edge. Passing into pasture, head half right to a final stile in the far corner to come out on to a lane.

❽ Go left and then right by the entrance to Potterton Park to reach another junction. Turn left down Potterton Lane, which eventually leads back to Barwick.

WHERE TO EAT AND DRINK The Gascoigne Arms and the Black Swan lie in the centre of Barwick, close to the maypole. The Arabian Horse in Aberford is another good place for lunch.

WHAT TO SEE Over the A1(M) from Aberford, 14th-century Lead Church is all that's left of Lead, one of Yorkshire's 'lost' villages.

Stanley Ferry and its surrounding waterways

DISTANCE 7.5 miles (12.1km)	MINIMUM TIME 2hrs 30min

ASCENT/GRADIENT 279ft (85m) ▲▲▲   LEVEL OF DIFFICULTY ✦✦✦

PATHS Canal tow path and other good paths, no stiles

LANDSCAPE Flat land and reclaimed colliery works

SUGGESTED MAP OS Explorer 289 Leeds

START/FINISH Grid reference: SE354230

DOG FRIENDLINESS Can be off lead on tow path

PARKING Large car park at Stanley Ferry Marina

PUBLIC TOILETS None on route

As with the coal industry, the Yorkshire woollen industry was held back by the high costs of transporting its goods to ships bound for European markets. The river system provided a solution for both.

THE AIRE AND CALDER NAVIGATION

The River Calder meandered circuitously through the flat landscape to the east of Wakefield. In 1699 William III authorised the Aire and Calder rivers to be made navigable to the tidal Ouse. Leeds and Wakefield wool merchants paid for the canalising and deepening of parts of the rivers. The Aire and Calder Navigation took a more direct route, with comparatively few locks, so both costs and journey times were cut significantly. The first large vessels reached Leeds Bridge in 1700 and Wakefield the following year.

The Aire and Calder Navigation proved to be a profitable investment for all concerned and continued to be upgraded to allow ever-larger vessels to negotiate the locks. It is still used for commercial traffic today.

There are two aqueducts, side by side, at Stanley Ferry. The older aqueduct, built (1836–1839) for the Aire and Calder Navigation Company, is believed to have been the first such suspension bridge in the world. It's a fine, cast iron trough structure, suspended from cast-iron arches. The new aqueduct, a concrete structure, dates from 1981.

About 1860 a new system was invented for bulk transportation of coal by canal. Floating tubs, each one capable of holding up to 10 tons of coal, were linked together and pulled by steam tugs. Once at the port, these tubs, known as Tom Puddings, were lifted by primitive hoists and their contents emptied into ships' holds. This idea was refined by hauliers on the Aire and Calder Navigation, who developed tubs capable of carrying heavier loads, and hydraulic machines for loading and unloading. The tubs were a common sight on the waterway.

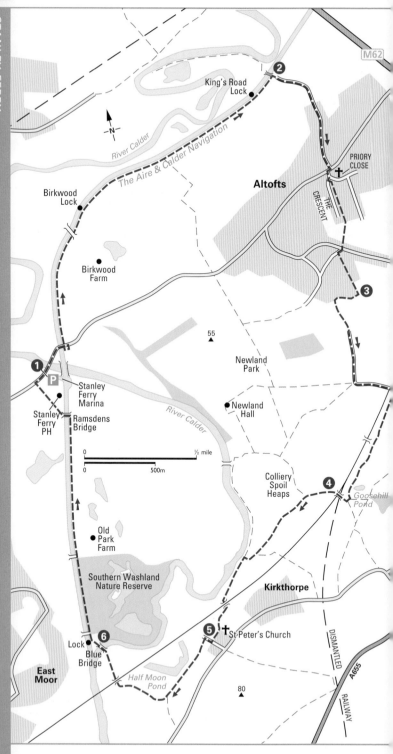

King's Road Lock

M62

Altofts

PRIORY CLOSE

THE CRESCENT

Birkwood Lock

River Calder

The Aire & Calder Navigation

Birkwood Farm

3

55 ▲

Newland Park

1 P Stanley Ferry Marina

Stanley Ferry PH

Ramsdens Bridge

River Calder

Newland Hall

0   ½ mile
0   500m

Old Park Farm

Colliery Spoil Heaps

4 Goosehill Pond

Kirkthorpe

Southern Washland Nature Reserve

DISMANTLED

Lock

6 Blue Bridge

East Moor

5 † St Peter's Church

Half Moon Pond

80 ▲

A655 RAILWAY

1 Park at the Stanley Ferry Marina. Turn right along the road, which crosses first the River Calder, then the canal: the Aire and Calder Navigation. Take steps to the right, immediately after the canal, to follow the tow path to the right, back under the road bridge. Walk beneath another bridge at Birkwood Lock. Beyond King's Road Lock you come to a canal bridge and a lane to the right.

2 Follow the lane right for 0.5 miles (800m) to the main road at Altofts opposite St Mary's Church. Go right and left into The Crescent. After 50yds (46m), at the junction with Priory Close, take a ginnel between the houses opposite. At the end, bear right across a playing field and follow a street out to a junction. Take the street diagonally opposite beside a chemist, leaving left after only a few yards down another passage between house backs. Keep ahead beyond its end to emerge into a field.

3 Go right to the corner and swing left opposite a cul-de-sac through a kissing gate onto a contained path between the fields. Beyond a stream, continue beside another field and keep ahead over a rise to meet a rough track. Go forward and then left across a railway line. Immediately after the bridge, turn right onto a grass path, passing beneath an electricity pylon. Over an access road carry on to pick up a developing path that winds into trees. Passing Goosehill Pond, fork up right to emerge onto a drive. Turn right, walking through gateposts at Goosehill Cattery to cross a couple of railway bridges.

4 Keep ahead along a broad gravel track, signed 'Pennine Trail'. When the track later fragments by a gate, bear left but then later on fork right, the onward path contouring the scrubby hillside and eventually reaching a junction overlooking the River Calder. Swing left, dropping to a small stone bridge across a stream. Carry on, going left again on a track that then leads beneath a railway bridge. Soon passing through a gate, wind on behind Kirkthorpe Hall and past the church, forking right to emerge onto the lane at Kirkthorpe.

5 Turn right, but then after 50yds (46m), go left on a track that soon narrows to a woodland path. Remain with the main path above Half Moon Pond to a fork by an information board. Bear right through a gate (signed 'Stanley Ferry'), negotiating a wooded dip to gain the top of an embankment. Go right, walking for 0.25 miles (400m) before dropping right to pass beneath the railway again. A good track leads to the Blue Bridge, which spans the River Calder beside a lock that begins the Aire and Calder Navigation.

6 Walk on to a junction by a canal bridge and fork down left to follow the tow path away to the north. At the next bridge, the track above leads into the Southern Washland Nature Reserve. Continue beside the canal to Ramsdens Bridge, crossing to return past the pub to the car park.

WHERE TO EAT AND DRINK You can enjoy good food and a relaxing drink at the canalside Stanley Ferry pub.

Overleaf: All Hallows Church, Bardsey (Walk 8)

Bardsey and Pompocali

DISTANCE 3 miles (4.8km)   MINIMUM TIME 1hr 15min

ASCENT/GRADIENT 246ft (75m) ▲▲▲   LEVEL OF DIFFICULTY ✦✦✦

PATHS Good paths and tracks (though some, being bridleways, may be muddy)

LANDSCAPE Arable and woodland

SUGGESTED MAP OS Explorer 289 Leeds

START/FINISH Grid reference: SE368432

DOG FRIENDLINESS Keep on lead by roads and in fields near livestock

PARKING Street parking off A58 at southern end of Bardsey

PUBLIC TOILETS None on route

The Romans built a network of important roads across Yorkshire and provided good transport links between their most important forts, such as Ilkley (probably their *Olicana*), Tadcaster (*Calcaria*) and York (*Eboracum*). And one of these roads, marked on old maps as Ryknield Street, passed close to the village of Bardsey. You walk a short stretch of the old Roman road when you take the track from Hetchell Wood.

STIRRING REMAINS

Adjacent to these woods (on the Ordnance Survey map as Pompocali), are a set of intriguing, if overgrown, earthworks. A number of Roman finds have been unearthed here, including a quern for grinding corn and a stone altar dedicated to the god Apollo. A few miles away (3.2km), at Dalton Parlours, the site of a large Roman villa has been discovered.

Once the Romans had abandoned this northern outpost of their empire, Bardsey became part of the kingdom of Elmet, and by the 13th century the village had been given to the monks of Kirkstall Abbey. After the Dissolution of Monasteries, in 1539, Bardsey came under the control of powerful local families – notably the Lords Bingley. The Parish Church of All Hallows, visited towards the end of this walk, is an antiquity – part of the building is Anglo Saxon.

Above the church is a grassy mound, where a castle once stood. Some of the stonework from the castle was incorporated into the fabric of Bardsey Grange, whose most notable inhabitant was William Congreve. Born here in 1670, Congreve went on to write a number of Restoration comedies, such as *The Way of the World.*

Close to the city, yet with its own identity, Bardsey has expanded beyond its ancient centre to become a popular commuter village for people who work in Leeds. It joins a group of places that lay claim to having the country's oldest pub. The Bingley Arms has better claims than most; there is documentary evidence of brewers and innkeepers going back a thousand years. Bardsey is, in short, a historic little spot.

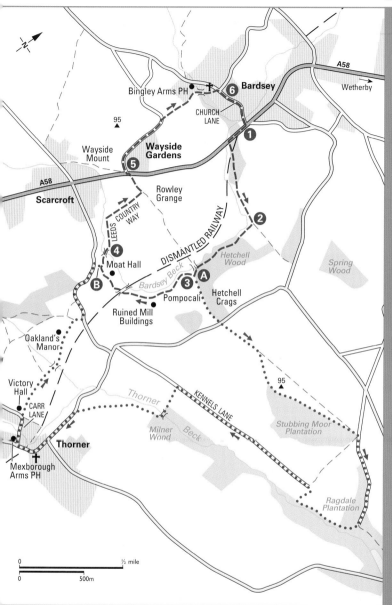

① Begin from the junction of Church Lane with the A58 and head south along the main road. After 150yds (137m), take a path off left beside a gate into a wood. It rises to the overgrown embankment of the former Leeds–Wetherby Railway, which opened in 1876 and operated until 1964, when it fell victim with many other railway lines to Dr. Beeching's cuts. Go right and almost immediately left through a gap. Soon emerging into a field, continue beside the perimeter. Passing into a second field keep with the boundary as it swings right down to more trees.

2 Pass through a kissing gate into Hetchell Wood Nature Reserve. Keep right where the path later forks, soon passing beneath Hetchell Crags, whose soft gritstone facade offers a challenge to local climbers. Leave the reserve through another kissing gate at a junction by a footbridge spanning Bardsey Beck. Turn left along a climbing track that was once part of a Roman road. Look for a bridleway signed off through a gate, a short distance along on the right.

3 Through the gate, a path leads away above the stream, skirting the Roman earthworks (Pompocali on the OS map). Beyond an overhanging rock, the path rises to a junction (to the left, you can wander back to investigate these intriguing mounds). The onward path, however, keeps to the right, joining a track that shortly leads past ruinous mill buildings. Carry on beneath an old railway bridge and across a stream. Wind around two sides of a paddock and then swing left along a drive coming from Moat Hall. Look for a stile breaking the right-hand wall, a few paces along on the right.

4 Take a field-edge path, with a hedge to the right (from here back to Bardsey you are walking the Leeds Country Way). Towards the far end of the field, your path turns right into a copse. Cross a beck on a little wooden footbridge and swing left through scrub above the stream. Shortly wind right to emerge into the corner of a field. Climb away beside the right-hand hedge, dropping beyond the crest of the hill to a junction. Go left here on a track that follows a broken wall to meet the A58 road.

5 Walk left for just 20yds (18m) and turn right into Wayside Mount; an unsurfaced access road serves a collection of detached houses. Beyond the last house go through a gateway and follow the track ahead, a tall hedge on your left. When the track later swings left, leave and walk ahead, ignoring a stile to follow the field-edge downhill. Approaching the bottom, bear right across the field corner to find a path dropping into the trees below. Cross a stream and climb to a gate into the churchyard. Keep right of the church to meet a road.

6 Go right on Church Lane to return to the start point.

WHERE TO EAT AND DRINK The Bingley Arms, in Bardsey, offers excellent food and, in summer, barbecues on the terrace. Parts of the pub are supposed to date back to the year 950, when it was known as the Priests Inn.

WHAT TO SEE Bardsey's church was built in Anglo-Saxon times: just the nave we see today. Over the next thousand years the old Saxon porch was extended into a bell tower, aisles were added in Norman times and, in the 19th century, the nave walls were heightened to support a new roof.

Bardsey and Thorner

DISTANCE 7.5 miles (12.1km)   MINIMUM TIME 2hrs 45min

ASCENT/GRADIENT 640ft (195m) ▲▲▲   LEVEL OF DIFFICULTY ✚✚✚

SEE MAP AND INFORMATION PANEL FOR WALK 8

From Point **Ⓐ**, keep walking up the sunken track with the Roman earthworks hidden to your right. Go through a gate and cross a minor road, squeezing past a gate to the ongoing path, which continues at the field-edge. Entering Stubbing Moor Plantation, the path swings left to run within the boundary. At the far end, bear right on a farm track and, after 20yds (18m), keep left at a fork. Follow this path for almost 0.5 miles (800m) through Ragdale Plantation to a junction and turn right, soon following a stream.

After 0.25 miles (400m), watch for the signed bridlepath swinging right to climb away at the edge of a field. At the top, turn left, passing through a gate to continue along a hedged track, Kennels Lane. Pass a barn and walk for another 0.5 miles (800m) to find a footpath signed through a gap on the left to Thorner via Jubilee Bridge. Follow the hedge on your right into the valley, where a stepped path drops through the trees to a bridge over the stream. Turn right, briefly following the beck before climbing to a stile leaving the wood. Keep on the path ahead, rising across the slope of the hill. Join a hedge, continuing beyond its end to a stile.

Cross and continue above the right-hand hedge for some 300yds (274m) to a kissing gate, through which, drop out to a road by a house. Go left to a T-junction in Thorner, there turning right to pass the parish church.

About 150yds (137m) past the church, and immediately before the Mexborough Arms, turn right into Carr Lane. When the road bends left past a junction, continue ahead along a track that leaves beside Thorner Victory Hall (the onward route now accompanies the Leeds Country Way back to Bardsey). Take two kissing gates in quick succession and continue along a hedged path between fields over the shoulder of a rise. Through a kissing gate at the bottom of a dip beyond, cross a beck and walk up the next field to find a stile near the top-left corner. To the right, a contained path runs past Oaklands Manor, coming out beside the lodges. Turn right to a junction and then left in front of a large, stone farmhouse.

Follow this road downhill. After crossing a stream, continue uphill for 100yds (91m) before turning off along a gravel track beside a white-painted house. Just before the gate to Moat Hall, take a stile on your left (Point **Ⓑ**) to rejoin Walk 8.

The lakes of Walton Heronry

DISTANCE 3.5 miles (5.7km)	MINIMUM TIME 1hr 15min

ASCENT/GRADIENT 197ft (60m) ▲▲▲   LEVEL OF DIFFICULTY ✚✚✚

PATHS Good paths and tracks throughout, canal tow path, no stiles

LANDSCAPE Country park, lakes, woodland and canal

SUGGESTED MAP OS Explorer 278 Sheffield & Barnsley

START/FINISH Grid reference: SE375153

DOG FRIENDLINESS Good, but care should be taken when near wildfowl

PARKING Anglers Country Park on Haw Park Lane, between Crofton and Ryehill

PUBLIC TOILETS At the visitor centre, at start of walk

Few houses are situated as delightfully as Walton Hall, isolated upon a little lake island with just a cast iron bridge for access. It was the ancestral home of Charles Waterton, who deserves wider acclaim, for although he was at the time regarded as an eccentric, his environmental interests and ideas would have put him in the vanguard of 'green' thinking today.

A MAN AHEAD OF HIS TIME

Born in 1782, Charles Waterton developed a childhood interest in wildlife, but his passion flourished when he subsequently went to British Guyana to administer the family's sugar estates. During his time there he made several expeditions into the interior and neighbouring Brazil, becoming fascinated by South America's unusual wildlife. He returned home with many exotic specimens, many of which are now displayed in the Wakefield Museum, and turned his attention to studying and protecting his local wildlife.

At a time when shooting parties were an intrinsic part of landed gentry society, he created what was perhaps the world's first nature reserve, building a high wall around his estate to keep the poachers out. However, he opened the grounds for the peaceful enjoyment of local people. Over the next 40 years he fought against pollution, planted countless trees, managed his woodland for the benefit of the wildlife and built hides from which to watch the wild birds. He also experimented in encouraging breeding and is credited with the invention of the nesting box. One success was the establishment of herons on the estate; their descendants still around today. He spent over £9,000 (the equivalent £2.5 million today) on his project, funding it, he said, 'from the wine I do not drink'. When he died after a fall in

1865, he was buried in the woods he loved, a linnet supposedly singing as his coffin was lowered into the ground.

Ironically, his son Edmund subsequently resorted to hosting shooting parties to help to pay off his own debts. But the estate survived and today is split between a country park, nature reserve and a golf club, with the house forming the centrepiece of the four-star Waterton Park Hotel.

INDUSTRY TO COUNTRY PARK

Beyond the wood and parkland of Waterton's estate, areas of the country park have been reclaimed from industry. The main lake was once a vast, opencast coal pit surrounded by spoil heaps, while the two reservoirs to the south supplied the Barnsley Canal. Opened in 1799 to carry coal, the waterway later lost traffic to the railways and eventually closed in 1953. It was then returned to nature in the form of a country park. At the park's visitor centre you will find exhibitions illustrating Squire Waterton's work and highlighting the local wildlife.

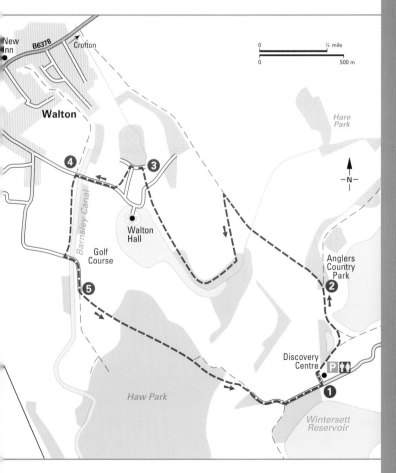

1 From the car park, take the track past the visitor centre towards the main lake, signed 'Lakeside Walk'. At a fork, bear left towards the bird hides. Keep to the main path for some 300yds (274m), looking for a gap in the left hedge from which a path is signed to Walton.

2 Through a kissing gate, walk at the edge of two fields towards the distant golf course. Cross a footbridge into a third field and keep ahead to another kissing gate in the far corner. Turn sharp left on a path fringing the golf course, passing a small pond to enter woodland. Ignoring a crossing path, keep to the obvious trail, which shortly curves right past the tail of a lake. Beyond the trees, continue forward as golfers' paths merge to reach a junction. Take the waymarked grass path ahead to a three-way fingerpost and carry on towards the Barnsley Canal, descending behind the hotel complex to meet a gravel drive.

3 Go left, but leave after 50yds (46m), going left again on a waymarked path that climbs beside a fence. At the top, pass through an opening in a high brick wall and swing left again to emerge onto the hotel's main drive. Follow it up to the right, rising to a bridge over the Barnsley Canal near the golf clubhouse.

4 Immediately over the bridge, drop left to the tow path and follow it away beside the disused waterway. After 0.25 miles (400m) bear off right, rising to another bridge over the canal. Cross and swing right in front of a gate on a broad track running above the opposite bank.

5 When it later forks, keep left beside the boundary wall of the Walton Estate into woodland. Eventually reaching a junction at the end of the wall, bear right with the main track. Walk on to a second junction by an information board and go left towards Anglers Country Park. Leaving Haw Park wood behind, the track later develops as a lane, eventually leading back to the car park and visitor centre.

WHERE TO EAT AND DRINK The New Inn at nearby Walton welcomes walkers. The regular menu and daily specials offer home-cooked food from Wednesday to Sunday that is locally sourced wherever possible. There's a good selection of wines and up to seven cask beers on tap to quench the fiercest thirst. Closer to hand is Squires Tea Room in the visitor centre by the car park.

WHAT TO SEE In a heronry, it makes sense to look out for herons. The tall, grey heron is one of Britain's most easily recognised birds. At one time it was believed the heron's skill at catching fish must be due to magical substances in its legs.

WHILE YOU'RE THERE Nearby Nostell Priory is a magnificent house built in 1733 on the site of a medieval priory. It is home to art treasures, paintings and tapestries – with a particularly fine collection of Chippendale furniture. There are extensive grounds and gardens, with a scented rose garden and peaceful lakeside walks.

Harewood and around the Harewood Estate

DISTANCE 7 miles (11.3km)	MINIMUM TIME 2hrs 30min

ASCENT/GRADIENT 672ft (205m) ▲▲▲   LEVEL OF DIFFICULTY ✚✚✚

PATHS Good paths and parkland tracks all the way

LANDSCAPE Arable and parkland

SUGGESTED MAP OS Explorer 289 Leeds or 297 Lower Wharfedale

START/FINISH Grid reference: SE334450

DOG FRIENDLINESS Keep on lead in conservation areas, near sheep and deer and on roads

PARKING Limited in Harewood village. From traffic lights, take A659, and park in first lay-by on left

PUBLIC TOILETS None on route; in Harewood House if you pay to go in

The grand old houses of West Yorkshire tend to be in the form of 'Halifax' houses (such as East Riddlesden Hall). Self-made yeomen and merchant clothiers built their mansions to show the world that they'd made their 'brass'. But Harewood House, on the edge of Leeds, is more ambitious, and is still one of the great treasure houses of England.

VISION INTO REALITY

The Harewood Estate passed through a number of wealthy hands during the 16th and 17th centuries, eventually being bought by the Lascelles family who still own the house today. Edwin Lascelles left the 12th-century castle in its ruinous state, to overlook the broad valley of the River Wharfe, but demolished the old hall. He wanted to create something very special in its place and hired the best architects and designers to turn his vision into grand reality.

John Carr of York created a veritable palace of a house, in an imposing neoclassical style and laid out the estate village of Harewood too. The interior of the building was designed by Robert Adam, and Thomas Chippendale made furniture for every room. The foundations were laid in 1759; 12 years later the house was finished. Inside the house are paintings by JMW Turner and Thomas Girtin, who both painted at the house. The sumptuous interior, however, is in sharp contrast to the world of those below stairs, whose life and work is depicted in the Old Kitchen and servants' quarters.

The house sits in extensive grounds, shaped by Lancelot 'Capability' Brown, the most renowned designer of the English landscape. In addition to the formal gardens, he created the lake and the woodland paths you take on this walk. The gardens are now also used for events throughout the year to help Harewood House earn its keep.

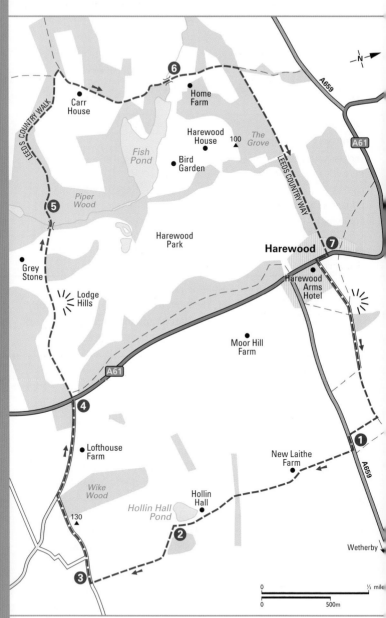

1 From the lay-by walk 50yds (46m) away from the village of Harewood, cross the road and walk right down the access track to New Laithe Farm.

Pass left of the farm buildings to pick up a gravel track heading into the valley bottom. Go through a gate and bear half left up a field, towards Hollin

Hall. Keep left of the buildings to pass Hollin Hall Pond.

② Beyond the pond, swing left around the corner of Spring Wood and follow a track at the field-edge to reach the top corner. Go through gates and continue up the hill, the track later becoming enclosed and ending at a junction.

③ Go right along the crest of the hill to have easy, level walking on an enclosed sandy track (now following the Leeds Country Way). Keep straight ahead past a junction, through a gate. Skirt woodland to emerge onto a lane. Follow it right to reach the A61.

④ Cross the road to enter the Harewood Estate (via the right-hand gate, between imposing gateposts). Follow the broad track ahead, through landscaped parkland, soon getting views of Harewood House to the right. Enter woodland through a gate, turning immediately left after you reach a stone bridge.

⑤ After 100yds (91m), bear right at a fork and keep with the main track.

It later swings right, dipping across a stream and eventually reaching a crossing. Go right down to another junction and turn right again, the way curving left out of the trees to pass Carr House. Carry on at the edge of the park, then swing left again at the next junction, rising beside a high wall to meet a metalled drive. Bear left to a crossroads and keep ahead over a bridge and another crossing, climbing beside the Home Farm complex.

⑥ Follow the drive into the deer park, keeping right at the next junction. Continue through woodland until you come to the few houses that comprise the estate village of Harewood.

⑦ Cross the main A61 road and walk right, for 50yds (46m), to take a metalled drive just before the Harewood Arms Hotel. Beyond Maltkiln House, the way continues as a gated field track, with views over Lower Wharfedale. Carry on through a second gate for a further 350yds (320m) to a junction and go right over a cattle grid along a permissive bridleway, regaining the A659 beside the lay-by.

WHERE TO EAT AND DRINK Almost opposite the main gates of Harewood House is the Harewood Arms Hotel, a former coaching inn that offers the chance of a drink or meal towards the end of the walk and a beer garden in case of good weather.

WHAT TO SEE The red kite, a beautiful fork-tailed bird of prey, is once again becoming a familiar sight. Centuries of persecution had brought them close to extinction in England, but Harewood has successfully re-introduced them to this part of Yorkshire. Now, during winter and spring, up to 80 birds can gather as evening falls.

WHILE YOU'RE THERE As well as the house there are endless paths amongst the terraces and gardens to explore. There is also much to see in the bird garden, which houses exotic and rare species from around the world.

Rural Leeds and the Meanwood Valley

DISTANCE 5 miles (8km)	MINIMUM TIME 2hrs

ASCENT/GRADIENT 541ft (165m) ▲▲▲   LEVEL OF DIFFICULTY ✚✚✚

PATHS Urban ginnels, parkland and woodland paths

LANDSCAPE Mostly woodland

SUGGESTED MAP OS Explorers 289 Leeds, 297 Lower Wharfedale

START Grid reference: SE293350

FINISH Grid reference: SE270402

DOG FRIENDLINESS Keep on lead near roads

PARKING Street parking off main road at both ends of the walk; bus services 1 and X84 operate between the two points

PUBLIC TOILETS None on route

This is a splendid ramble, surprisingly rural in aspect throughout, even though it begins just a stone's throw from the bustling heart of Leeds. You start among the terraces of red-brick houses that are so typical of the city, and five minutes later you are in delightful woodland.

LINKING WITH THE DALES WAY

The walk follows the first 5 miles (8km) of the Dales Way link path from Leeds to Ilkley (the walk's official starting point). The link path begins at Woodhouse Moor and follows Woodhouse Ridge into Meanwood Park and along the Meanwood Valley. The route is also promoted as the Meanwood Valley Trail and there are regular waymarkers.

PARKLIFE

Leeds has many parks within the city limits: long established green spaces such as Roundhay Park, and newer parks created from 'brownfield' sites. The first few miles of this walk are through some of this pleasant parkland, then, having crossed beneath the Leeds Ring Road, you enter the more natural surroundings of Adel Woods. The walk finishes near Adel church, dedicated to St John the Baptist. Though small, it is one of the most perfectly proportioned Norman churches in the country. The ornamental stone carving is noteworthy – especially the four arches framing the doorway.

From Adel, there's a reliable bus service back to Woodhouse Moor. To extend the walk by 1.5 miles (2.4km), don't turn left down Stair Foot Lane (at Point **Ⓐ**), but take the track ahead, and turn left when you come to King Lane. This brings you to Golden Acre Park, near Bramhope (on the X84 bus route for getting back to Leeds).

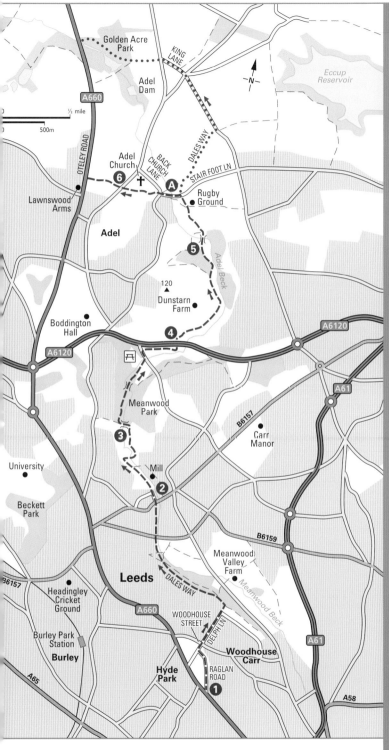

Golden Acre Park

KING LANE

Eccup Reservoir

Adel Dam

A660

½ mile

500m

OTELEY ROAD

DALES WAY

Adel Church

BACK CHURCH LANE

STAIR FOOT LN

6 †

A

Rugby Ground

Lawnswood Arms

Adel

5

Adel Beck

120 ▲

Dunstarn Farm

4

A6120

Boddington Hall

A6120

A61

Meanwood Park

B6157

Carr Manor

University

3

Beckett Park

Mill

2

Meanwood Valley Farm

B6159

Leeds

DALES WAY

Meanwood Beck

A61

B6157

Headingley Cricket Ground

A660

WOODHOUSE STREET

DELPH LN

Woodhouse Carr

A61

Burley Park Station

Burley

Hyde Park

RAGLAN ROAD

1

A65

A58

1 Walk down Raglan Road (opposite the library at the corner of Hyde Park) and on along Cathcart Street. At the T-junction, turn right onto Rampart Road, cross Woodhouse Street, and walk ahead up Delph Lane. At its ultimate end, go forward through a gap and left onto the higher path along Woodhouse Ridge. Keep with the main trail to a barrier. Where it splits, take the middle option to Grove Lane. There, cross to the path opposite, which shortly emerges at Monkbridge Road.

2 Cross the road into Highbury Lane, recovering the path beside Meanwood Beck beyond its end. At a junction by a converted mill, go left and then right onto a path between allotments. Keep on to emerge onto a street and walk ahead. After 100yds (91m), by a post box, turn right into Meanwood Park. Follow the drive to reach a car park. Pass through and swing left onto a lane that leads to a terrace of stone cottages, Hustlers Row.

3 Approaching the houses drop left along a stony track to cross a footbridge over Meanwood Beck. Bear right just beyond at a fork and head upstream above the beck, shortly rising to continue along a raised bank beside a disused mill leat. Ignoring side paths, it eventually leads to a pair of bridges. Swing over that on the right above a weir and walk forward to a broad path. Go left to emerge from the trees through a gate. Carry on at the edge of a field into more trees, ultimately coming out by a picnic site and information board onto a lane. Follow the lane left

but, just before reaching a junction with a main road, turn off along an unmarked track on the right. It runs below the embankment before swinging through an underpass.

4 Take steps, at the far end, on to a path that follows Adel Beck. Keep left of the next pile of boulders, rising to a path along the fringe of the woodland. Keep to this higher path until you eventually reach a major fork. Bear right, following an aqueduct across the dip of the valley. Curving left, the path continues through Adel Woods, in time meeting a prominent junction.

5 The Meanwood Valley Trail is signed left, dropping across a stone slab bridge and climbing steps to a small pond. Cross the small feeder stream and fork right. Occasional wayposts mark the ongoing path, which shortly emerges to run at the edge of more open ground. Joining a broader path keep left, finally emerging through a car park onto Stair Foot Lane. Go left, dropping through a dip and up to a junction. Turn right along Back Church Lane but, as that then bears right, keep ahead along a path to Adel church.

6 Walk past the church and leave the churchyard by a collection of coffins and millstones. Cross the road and take a field path opposite. Bear half left across the next field to the Otley Road (A660). Turn left to find a bus stop, opposite the Lawnswood Arms, for the bus back to Woodhouse Moor, in Leeds.

WHERE TO EAT AND DRINK There are several pubs just off route during this walk or the Lawnswood Arms at the finishing point.

Golden Acre Park and Breary Marsh

DISTANCE 5.5 miles (8.8km)	MINIMUM TIME 2hrs

ASCENT/GRADIENT 246ft (75m) ▲▲▲   LEVEL OF DIFFICULTY ✦✦✦

PATHS Good paths, tracks and quiet roads, several stiles

LANDSCAPE Parkland, woods and arable country

SUGGESTED MAP OS Explorer 297 Lower Wharfedale

START/FINISH Grid reference: SE266417

DOG FRIENDLINESS Keep on lead in park, along lanes and near livestock

PARKING Golden Acre Park car park, across road from park itself, on A660 just south of Bramhope

PUBLIC TOILETS Golden Acre Park, at start of walk

Leeds is fortunate to have so many green spaces. Some, like Roundhay Park, are long established; others, like the Kirkstall Valley nature reserve, have been created from post-industrial wasteland. But none have had a more chequered history than Golden Acre Park, 6 miles (9.7km) north of the city on the main A660.

AMUSEMENT PARK

The park originally opened in 1932 as an amusement park. The attractions included a miniature railway, nearly 2 miles (3.2km) in length, complete with dining car. The lake was the centre of much activity, with motor launches, dinghies for hire and races by the Yorkshire Hydroplane Racing Squadron. An open-air lido offered unheated swimming and The Winter Gardens Dance Hall boasted that it had 'the largest dance floor in Yorkshire'.

Visitors initially flocked to Golden Acre Park, but by the end of the 1938 season the amusement park had closed down and was sold to Leeds City Council. The site was subsequently transformed into botanical gardens – a process that's continued ever since. The hillside overlooking the lake has been lovingly planted with trees and unusual plants, including rock gardens and fine displays of rhododendrons.

The boats are long gone; the lake is now a haven for wildfowl. Within these 127 acres (51ha) is a wide variety of wildlife habitats, from open heathland to an old quarry. Lovers of birds, trees and flowers will find plenty to interest them at every season of the year. One of the few echoes of the original Golden Acre Park is a cafe near the entrance.

A car park has been built on the opposite side of the main road, with pedestrian access to the park via a tunnel beneath the road. Accessible to all, wheelchair users can make a circuit of the lake on a broad path.

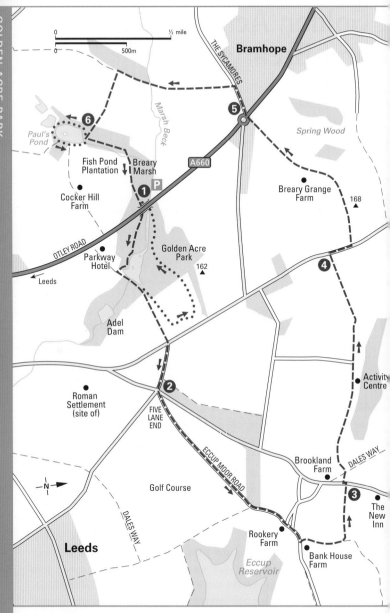

0 ————— ½ mile
0 ————— 500m

Bramhope

THE SYCAMORES

Marsh Beck

Spring Wood

6 Paul's Pond

Fish Pond Plantation

Breary Marsh

1 P

Cocker Hill Farm

A660

Breary Grange Farm

168 ▲

OTLEY ROAD

Parkway Hotel

Golden Acre Park

162 ▲

4

← Leeds

Adel Dam

Roman Settlement (site of)

2

FIVE LANE END

Activity Centre

ECCUP MOOR ROAD

Brookland Farm

DALES WAY

←—N—→

Golf Course

DALES WAY

3

The New Inn

Leeds

Rookery Farm

Bank House Farm

Eccup Reservoir

---

1 From the southern corner of the car park, an underpass leads into Golden Acre Park. Turn right on a path that winds to the far end of the lake. Ignore the path off left across the lake dam and walk forward out of the park onto a crossing tree-lined bridlepath. Go left beside the park boundary to

emerge at a junction of lanes. Take the one ahead, up to the aptly-named Five Lane End.

2 Take the second road on the left (Eccup Moor Road). Stick with it for a mile (1.6km) past junctions until you reach the outbuildings of Bank House

Farm, where a waymarked bridleway leaves on the left. It soon narrows to a hedged path. About 50yds (46m) before the footpath later swings right, take a stile in the fence on your left. Follow the field edge away to a wall stile and continue forward across another field to emerge onto a lane (The New Inn is then just along to your right).

3 Go left along the road for just 20yds (18m) to take a stile on your right. Keep ahead over an intersection to join another track, which leads forward to a gate and stile. Carry on for 150yds (137m) by the boundary to a waypost and bear right across the pasture to a stile in the end wall. Walk on towards an activity centre, bypassing it through a couple of kissing gates to meet a track. Go right and immediately left along an enclosed grass track past a donkey sanctuary. When it finishes, maintain your direction walking beside successive fields to reach a road.

4 Go right for 150yds (138m) then take a waymarked kissing gate on the left. Follow the field-edge path by the left fence. Beyond two more kissing gates bear left across another field behind Breary Grange Farm to a ladder stile beyond a large oak. Maintain the same direction to stile at the far corner and continue across a final field. Leave over a stile next to buildings onto the A660 by a roundabout.

5 Cross the main road and turn into The Sycamores. Walk past the Rugby Club, but some 100yds (91m) further on, leave through a kissing gate on the left. Head away at the edge of successive fields towards a wood. Crossing a beck, carry on beside the trees. Reaching a stile, swing left along a track towards a farmhouse. Continue on the field path beyond to a gate that leads into the Breary Marsh Nature Reserve.

6 The path off sharp right makes a circuit around the lake, a pleasant extension if you're not pushed for time. Otherwise, bear slightly right on a path below the foot of the dam. At a junction, go left with the Leeds Country Way, signed towards the A660. Wind with the bridleway across a bridge, but at the next junction, turn left back to the car park.

WHERE TO EAT AND DRINK It requires the shortest of detours, at about the halfway point of this walk, to visit The New Inn, near Eccup. A sign welcomes walkers and an extensive menu will whet your appetite. Within Golden Acre Park, you'll find the Bakery Coffee House, offering everything from a snack to a full meal.

WHAT TO SEE Look for the damp-loving alder trees in Breary Marsh. During winter you should see little siskins (a type of finch). You may also spy the vivid caterpillar of the alder moth.

WHILE YOU'RE THERE Bramhope's Puritan Chapel, adjacent to the entrance to the Britannia Hotel on the A660, was built in 1649, by devout Puritan Robert Dyneley. Peer through the windows to see its original furnishings, including box-pews and a three-deck pulpit.

Around Golden Acre Park

DISTANCE 3 miles (4.8km)   MINIMUM TIME 1hr

ASCENT/GRADIENT 213ft (65m) ▲▲▲   LEVEL OF DIFFICULTY ✚✚✚

SEE MAP AND INFORMATION PANEL FOR WALK 13

Golden Acre Park is justifiably popular with people who live to the north of Leeds. A short walk around the park can be taken, following the waymarked trails, or just wandering freely. You can make a pleasant circuit by following Walk 13 to the far side of the lake, then cross the dam to wander back through the delightful Heather Garden, Arboretum and Lilac Collection to the more formal gardens by the cafe.

The park offers a variety of habitats for attracting birds. The lake is the most obvious focus, with a resident flock of waterfowl. An identification board will help you to put names to the ducks, geese, gulls and swans that come to feed on visitors' bread. Other, rarer species may also be seen. Great crested grebes perform elaborate mating rituals during the nesting season. Whooper swans fly down from Scandinavia to winter here. During the spring and autumn migration, many species of water birds make fleeting visits.

The sloping woodlands, criss-crossed by paths, are the ideal habitat for woodpeckers, nuthatches and treecreepers. In summer, these trees are filled with songbirds, including many melodious species of warbler.

At the highest point of the park is an old quarry; look here for rock pipits and wagtails. An area of heathland, bursting with colour each summer from flowering gorse bushes, is where you will find linnets, yellowhammers and the fluid song of the skylark. In the more formal gardens, near the park's main entrance, you can see garden birds such as blue tits, chaffinches and robins. There is probably nowhere else in West Yorkshire where you could spot so many species of birds in such a small area. This is all the more remarkable when you consider that Golden Acre Park lies within the city boundary of Leeds.

Beside the car park is Breary Marsh. This is one of West Yorkshire's few remaining wetlands: an area of alder wood, with uncommon damp-loving plants, such as tussock sedge and marsh marigold. Access to the site is via a duck-boarded path beginning by the underpass; information panels help to identify the flora and fauna. At its end, go right through the woods to a bridge and follow a stream up to Paul's Pond. From the path around its bank you might spot a heron or a moorhen – before returning, by the same route, to the car park.

Around Newmillerdam

DISTANCE 4.5 miles (7.2km)   MINIMUM TIME 1hr 45min

ASCENT/GRADIENT 328ft (100m) ▲▲▲   LEVEL OF DIFFICULTY ✛✛✛

PATHS Good paths by lake and through woodland

LANDSCAPE Reservoir, heath and woodland

SUGGESTED MAP OS Explorer 278 Sheffield & Barnsley

START/FINISH Grid reference: SE330157

DOG FRIENDLINESS Keep on lead beside roads

PARKING Pay-and-display car park at western end of dam, on A61 between Wakefield and Barnsley

PUBLIC TOILETS Near start of walk

Called Thurstonhaugh by Norse settlers, the area subsequently became part of a large medieval estate held by the Neviles until the 18th century. The lake is actually a mill pond and the place gained its present name in the 13th century with the construction of a new corn mill. The original mill is thought to have stood near the boathouse, but has seen several reincarnations before ending up in its present location in the 17th century after the lake had been extended to increase the head of water to drive the machinery. The mill continued to operate until 1960 and, although subsequently partly destroyed by a fire, still stands.

A HUNTING ESTATE

The Pilkingtons bought the estate in 1765 as a hunting preserve, and at one time nine keepers were employed to manage the game and prevent poaching. Each was housed in a separate lodge, two of which stand by the main entrance to the park.

The Pilkingtons also built the impressive lakeshore boathouse in 1820 to serve as a pavilion where the ladies could relax while watching their menfolk shoot wildfowl from punts. A grade II listed building, it has been restored and is now hired out as a meeting venue with a difference.

A LOCAL COUNTRY PARK

Wakefield Council bought the park in 1954 and opened it to the public. The 16th-century Chevet Hall at the heart of the estate, however, was affected by mining subsidence and demolished in the 1960s.

Today, the park is a popular haunt for local people who come to walk, fish, watch birds or just feed the ducks. The lake is surrounded by three woods containing a mixture of larch and pine as well as oak, beech, birch and sycamore. The beech date from the Pilkingtons' time as do clumps of rhododendron, which were planted as game cover. The majority of trees, however, date from the 1950s, planted as a commercial crop to provide timber for pit props. The softwoods and rhododendrons are now gradually being removed to allow a more diverse woodland that will benefit flowers and wildlife. Bluebells and wood anemone are beginning to carpet the understorey and birds such as tree creepers and long-tailed tits can be spotted amongst the branches or around the shore. Great crested grebe breed on the lake and insects flying above the water attract several species of bat to feed during summer evenings.

THE GIFT OF A LOCAL PHOTOGRAPHER

Nearby Seckar Wood was part of a separate estate. It was bought by local photographer Warner Gothard, who left it for the enjoyment of local people on his death in 1940. Encompassing heath, wood and wetland, it is now an SSSI and is rich in wildlife.

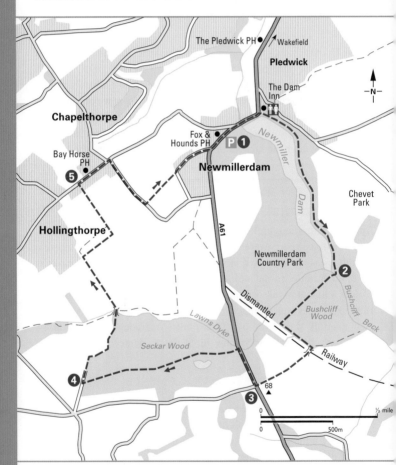

1 Turn right out of the car park and follow the main road down across the dam. At the far side, swing right in front of the Dam Inn through the park gates and follow the lakeside path. Ignore a causeway and carry on beyond the head of the lake to find a bridge across Bushcliff Beck.

2 On the far bank, go left and immediately right onto a path climbing into the trees. Keep with the main path to the crest of the hill, continuing ahead to a junction. Swing left on a broadening track, walking for 300yds (274m) to a major junction. Turn right, crossing a bridge over the disused Chevet branch line to follow a rough track out to the main road.

3 Cross and turn right, walking downhill for 350yds (320m) to find a barriered track leading left into Seckar Wood. Stick to the main path rising through the trees, ignoring a crossing and eventually emerging onto the edge of open heath. Keep going forward across the high ground to a belt of trees that appears on the far side, passing out through them onto a crossing track.

4 Follow the track right beside the wood, eventually crossing a stile and footbridge into the next field. Go right, passing through a gap in the corner of the field to then swing left beside the hedge. Approaching houses, turn right within the corner and follow the hedge down to a broad gap. Turn left on a field track that soon leads out onto the road at Chapelthorpe.

5 Walk right, passing the Bay Horse and then a junction to a mini-roundabout. There go right along Wood Lane for almost 0.25 miles (400m). After passing the Pennine Camphill Community, turn off left along a field path that leads through to the bend of a lane. Follow it ahead down to the A61 and turn left back to the car park.

WHERE TO EAT AND DRINK The Fox and Hounds, opposite the car park, offers a varied menu including snacks and has a good reputation for its food. The Dam Inn serves a daily carvery and is situated, appropriately, by the lake's dam. The Pledwick lies a little further along the main road towards Barnsley and it too has a welcoming restaurant.

WHAT TO SEE Ducks, geese and swans have no trouble finding food at Newmillerdam, as people with bagfulls of stale bread queue up to feed them. The most common of the ducks you'll see is the mallard, the 'basic' duck. The females are brown and make the satisfying 'quack quack' sounds which delight children. The males have distinctive green heads, yellow bills and grey bodies. Their tone is more nasal and much weaker sounding. Mallards pair off in the late autumn but the males leave egg incubation and rearing of the young to the females.

WHILE YOU'RE THERE Immediately to the north of Newmillerdam is Pugneys Country Park, a popular place of recreation with people from Wakefield. A large lake is overlooked by what remains of Sandal Castle. The original motte and bailey date from the 12th century, the later stone castle from the days of Richard III. He had planned to make Sandal Castle his key permanent stronghold in the north of England before he was killed at the Battle of Bosworth in 1485.

Tong and Fulneck's Moravian settlement

DISTANCE 5 miles (8km)	MINIMUM TIME 2hrs

ASCENT/GRADIENT 607ft (185m) ▲▲▲   LEVEL OF DIFFICULTY ✛✛✛

PATHS Ancient causeways, hollow ways and field paths

LANDSCAPE Mostly wooded valleys

SUGGESTED MAP OS Explorer 288 Bradford & Huddersfield

START/FINISH Grid reference: SE222306

DOG FRIENDLINESS Keep on lead across golf course and by livestock

PARKING Lay-by in Tong village, near village hall, or on edge of village

PUBLIC TOILETS None on route

FULNECK MORAVIAN SETTLEMENT

The Pennine areas of Yorkshire have long been strongholds for non-conformist faiths. The harsh conditions and uncertain livelihoods produced people who were both independent of mind and receptive to radical ideas. Some travelling preachers could fill churches, with congregations overflowing into the churchyard. The Revd William Grimshaw of Haworth was one such tireless orator. Religion was a passionate business in the 18th century and John Wesley found converts here, and austere Methodist chapels sprang up in many villages.

Just to the south of Pudsey is Fulneck, where another non-conformist church found a home. Pre-Reformation dissenters from the Roman Catholic Church, the Moravians, originated in Bohemia in the 15th century, and soon spread to Moravia. During the 18th century, Moravian missionaries were sent overseas to spread the word and one such group arrived in England. They were actually on their way to America, but a meeting with Benjamin Ingham, a Church of England clergyman, encouraged them to settle here.

In 1744 Ingham presented the Moravians with a 22-acre (9ha) estate for them to use as a centre for their work in Yorkshire. At first they called the settlement Lambshill then Fulneck, commemorating a town of that name in Moravia. The Moravians built some handsome buildings including a chapel, communal houses (for single brethren, single sisters and for widows), family houses, a shop, inn, bakery and workshops forming a close-knit, self-sufficient settlement. John Wesley visited Fulneck in 1780 and was impressed by their hard work.

Two schools were built (one for boys, one for girls) and these were eventually transformed into the fee-paying boarding schools that exist today. The most famous pupil was Richard Oastler who, in the 19th century, campaigned against 'child slavery' in Yorkshire's textile mills.

As close as it is to Pudsey, this terrace of splendid Georgian buildings has retained its air of separateness. The exposed site has discouraged further building, so what you see today is very much as the Moravians originally envisaged. Take the time to explore this evocative place and perhaps visit the museum (open Wednesday and Saturday afternoons), which explains the history of the Moravian Church and this unique Yorkshire outpost.

TONG AND COCKERS DALE

This short walk also takes you through two delightful valleys: Fulneck Valley and Cockers Dale. In these wooded dells, criss-crossed by ancient packhorse tracks and hollow ways, you feel a long way from the surrounding cities. On an attractive ridge between these valleys is the village of Tong (the name means 'a spit of land'), which has retained its traditional shape and character.

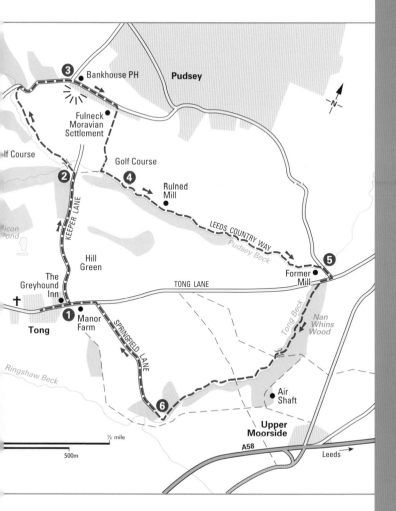

① From the village hall, walk down past the The Greyhound Inn and turn left into Keeper Lane. Becoming a track beyond a gate, it wends downhill to a footbridge below a confluence of streams.

② Cross and, ignoring the track ahead, swing left on the Leeds Country Way with the main beck on your left. Exiting a wood, keep ahead across a field. Leaving over a stile, turn sharp right up a path away from a bridge. Meeting a track, follow it right and later on, right again to come out on the bend of a lane opposite the Bankhouse pub.

③ Follow the road right past 20th-century housing into the Fulneck Moravian settlement. Just past Zachary's restaurant turn right beside the main school building, following a sign to Fulneck Golf Course. Keep right again but, passing the corner of the Robinson Building, watch for a stepped path leaving on the left. It heralds a delightful sunken lane that drops steeply within a dense line of trees across the golf course. Emerging at the bottom, cross a fairway to rejoin Pudsey Beck. Follow it left.

④ Leaving the golf course, keep going over stiles to a ruined mill. Dog-legging right and left, the path continues through a succession of fields and scrubland, straightening the course set by the accompanying squiggling beck. Finally, a walled path brings you out on to a lane.

⑤ Go right, past a converted mill, to a T-junction. Cross the main road and take a waymarked footpath between gateposts into Sykes' Wood. Immediately bear right, through a gap (signed 'Leeds Country Way'). Follow the path downhill, soon with Tong Beck. After walking about 0.5 miles (800m) through woodland, take a footbridge over the beck and bear left by the boundary up to a kissing gate. Follow a path along the edge of a field, then through woodland. Keep left, when the path eventually forks to a gate. Ignoring side paths, remain on this bank of the stream until you reach a kissing gate.

⑥ Through the gate, turn away from the river along a rising track called Springfield Lane. When you meet a road, go left to arrive back in Tong village.

WHERE TO EAT AND DRINK You have a choice of pubs on this short walk. The Greyhound Inn, in Tong, is a comfortable village inn with its own cricket pitch. The 17th-century building has beamed ceilings and a fine collection of antique toby jugs. Alternatively stop at the Bankhouse, on the approach to the Moravian Settlement at Fulneck.

WHILE YOU'RE THERE Immediately over the M62 you will find Oakwell Hall, dating from 1583. It is a splendid merchant clothier's house and retains many of its original Elizabethan features – not least the heavy oak panelling.

Burley in Wharfedale

DISTANCE 4.5 miles (7.2km)	MINIMUM TIME 2hrs

ASCENT/GRADIENT 754ft (230m) ▲▲▲   LEVEL OF DIFFICULTY ✦✦✦

PATHS Good tracks and moorland paths

LANDSCAPE Moor and arable land

SUGGESTED MAP OS Explorer 297 Lower Wharfedale

START/FINISH Grid reference: SE163458

DOG FRIENDLINESS Can be off lead but watch for grazing sheep

PARKING Roadside parking near station

PUBLIC TOILETS None on route

According to the legend, a giant by the name of Rombald used to live in these parts. While striding across the moor that now bears his name (in some versions of the story he was being chased by his angry wife) he dislodged a stone from a gritstone outcrop, and thus created the Calf, of the Cow and Calf rocks. Giants such as Rombald and Wade – and even the Devil himself – were apparently busy all over Yorkshire, dropping stones or creating big holes in the ground. It was perhaps an appealing way of accounting for some of the more unusual features of the landscape.

Rombalds Moor is pitted with old quarries, from which good quality stone was won. The impressive Cow and Calf rocks used to be a complete family unit, but the rock known as the Bull was broken up to provide building stone.

THE HERMIT OF ROMBALDS MOOR

At Burley Woodhead a public house called The Hermit commemorates Job Senior, a local character with a chequered career. Job worked as a farm labourer, before succumbing to the demon drink. He met an elderly widow of independent means, who lived in a cottage at Coldstream Beck and, thinking he might get his hands on her money and home, Job married the widow. Though she died soon after, Job took no profit. The family of her first husband pulled the cottage down, in Job's absence, leaving him homeless and penniless once more.

Enraged, he built himself a tiny hovel from the ruins of the house. Here he lived in filth and squalor on a diet of home-grown potatoes, which he roasted on a peat fire. He had long, lank hair, a matted beard and his legs were bandaged with straw.

His eccentric lifestyle soon had people flocking to see him. He offered weather predictions, and even advised visitors about their love lives. The possessor of a remarkable voice, he 'sang for his supper' as he lay on his bed of dried bracken and heather.

These impromptu performances encouraged Job to sing in nearby villages, and the theatres of Leeds and Bradford. Nevertheless, his unwashed appearance meant that he was forced to bed down in barns or outhouses. Eventually he was struck down with cholera and taken to Carlton Workhouse, where he died in 1857, aged 77. His life is commemorated in the old sign hanging over the entrance at The Hermit.

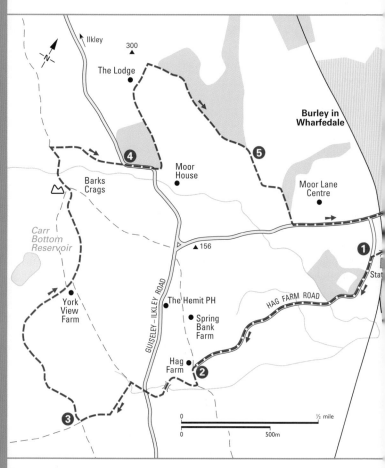

❶ From the station car park, cross the line via a footbridge and go left along a quiet lane. Follow the lane past houses and between fields up to Hag Farm.

❷ When the track wheels right, into the farmyard, keep left on a track to a stile and a gate. Follow a wall downhill for 100yds (91m) to a gap

stile in the wall. Don't pass through, but turn right, climbing beside a stream up to a stile. Carry on uphill, crossing two more stiles and then a footbridge across the stream. Continue up to cottages, winding out between them to meet the Guiseley-Ilkley road. (To visit The Hermit, go right here for 0.25 miles/400m.) Cross the road and continue on a stony track opposite. After 50yds (46m), leave left to ford a stream. Follow a path uphill through trees and then between walls to a gate. Turn right beside the wall, which soon curves away, leaving you heading upwards on a trod.

3 Meet a stony track and follow it to the right, along the moorland edge. Follow a wall to a stile by a gate. Immediately after, keep right when the track forks. Keep to the right again as you approach a small brick building. Route-finding is now easy, as the track wheels around a farm. At the next farm (called York View because on a clear day, you can see York Minster from here) branch left off the main track, gradually descending by a wall on your right. As you approach a third farm, look out for two barns and a gate, on the right. They stand opposite an indistinct path to the left, which curves around a small quarry. Enjoy level walking through bracken with great views over Lower Wharfedale. After 0.25 miles (400m), drop into a narrow ravine to cross Coldstone Beck. As you climb away, bear right and follow a path downhill to meet a road by a sharp bend.

4 Walk 100yds (91m) down the road to another sharp bend. Turn off along Stead Lane, a stony track which leads past several houses, to continue between the fields beyond. After passing a wooden chalet, leave the track as it swings left towards a farm, dropping through a kissing gate to the right. Walk away beside the wood on your left. Beyond another kissing gate, keep by the right-hand boundary, leaving at the far side to follow a fenced path ahead.

5 Reaching a track, go right, but after 200yds (183m), bear off left along a path which leads to a second track within trees. Follow it right to the road and go left back to the station.

WHERE TO EAT AND DRINK The Hermit is a welcoming stone-built pub in Burley Woodhead, whose name recalls an eccentric local character. During the walk it is easy to make a short detour to the inn, with its oak-panelled and beamed rooms and views of Wharfedale. Alternatively, the village of Burley in Wharfedale also boasts a number of places to get a bite to eat.

WHAT TO SEE Rombalds Moor is home to the red grouse, often claimed to be the only truly indigenous British bird. Grouse take off from their heather hiding places with heart-stopping suddenness, with their unmistakable and evocative cry of 'go back, go back, go back'. The moorland habitat is carefully managed to maintain a supply of young heather for the grouse to nest and feed in as grouse shooting is a lucrative business. The season begins on the 'Glorious Twelfth' of August.

WHILE YOU'RE THERE Ilkley's parish church, which can trace its origins to the 7th century, contains three beautiful Anglo-Saxon crosses. It occupies the site of a Roman fort overlooking the River Wharfe and, although only a short stretch of wall remains visible, many of the artefacts discovered during excavations can be seen in the nearby Manor House Museum. Other exhibits describe the wealth of prehistoric art scattered across the surrounding hillsides and explore Ilkley's growth over three centuries as a spa town. The impressive mullion-windowed building is interesting in its own right as one of the town's oldest buildings.

Around Farnley Tyas

DISTANCE 4.5 miles (7.2km)   MINIMUM TIME 1hr 45min

ASCENT/GRADIENT 804ft (245m) ▲▲▲   LEVEL OF DIFFICULTY ✦✦✦

PATHS Field paths, a little road walking on quiet lanes, several stiles

LANDSCAPE Arable, rolling countryside and woodland

SUGGESTED MAP OS Explorer 288 Bradford & Huddersfield

START/FINISH Grid reference: SE162125

DOG FRIENDLINESS Keep on lead near roads

PARKING Roadside parking in Farnley Tyas by recreation field

PUBLIC TOILETS None on route

Despite its proximity to Huddersfield, the area to the south of the town is surprisingly rural. As you gaze down into the Woodsome Valley from Farnley Tyas, you feel a long way from the mills and terraced houses that typify most of the county. Farnley Tyas and the fortification of Castle Hill face each other across the valley, and across the centuries. The village was mentioned in the Domesday Book, as 'Fereleia', but the history of Castle Hill extends at least 4,000 years. The site was inhabited by neolithic settlers who defended it with earth ramparts. Axe heads and other flint tools dating from this era and found here during archaeological digs are now displayed in Huddersfield's Tolson Museum. The Stone Age settlers were just the first of many peoples who saw the hill's defensive potential. Its exposed position, with uninterrupted views on all sides, made it an ideal place for a fortification.

Almost 900 years ago the de Lacy family built a motte-and-bailey castle here, having been given land as a reward for their part in the Norman Conquest. Though the structure was demolished in the 14th century, the site has been known ever since as Castle Hill. Most of the earthworks and ramparts that can be seen today date from medieval times.

The attractive hilltop village of Farnley Tyas gained its double-barrelled moniker to differentiate it from other Farnleys – one near Leeds, the other near Otley. The 'Tyas' suffix is the name of the area's most prominent family, who owned land here from the 13th century onwards.

THE GOLDEN COCK

Originally a farm, the pub has been at the centre of village life since the 17th century. During the 19th century, a group called the Royal Corkers used to ride over from Huddersfield to enjoy supper at the Golden Cock. Corks were placed on the dining table, with the last person (usually the only person!) to pick up a cork having to pay for supper for the whole party. Any newcomer to the group would unknowingly pick up a cork, thus leaving them to pay the bill.

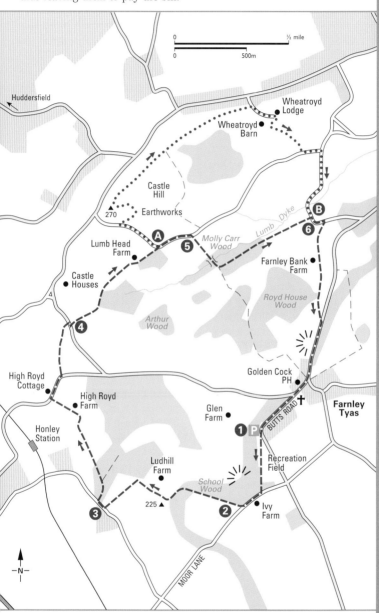

1 Enter the recreation field and walk away past a play area by the right wall. Beyond a second field, follow a walled track out to meet a road. Go right along Moor Lane.

2 After 100yds (91m), turn right down a walled track, with School Wood to your right. Leaving the trees, there is a view of Castle Hill ahead and beyond to Huddersfield. To the left is Meltham, with the uplands of Meltham Moor behind. When the track bends right for the second time, towards Ludhill Farm, drop left to a walled path. Walk downhill to take a stile next to a metal gate, strike left across a field to another stile, and bear right, descending more steeply through scrub. The way then swings left to accompany a sunken path down to meet a road.

3 Go right, downhill, but just after a small terrace of cottages, turn off right on a track into woodland. Some 50yds (46m) beyond a gate, bear left onto a narrow path that descends to a stile. Continue across a field, aiming towards a house on the opposite hillside. Cross a stream on stepping stones and walk up through a spur of woodland. Climb another field into the top corner, just left of the house. A contained path leads out to a drive, which climbs left to meet a road opposite High Royd Cottage. Follow the road right for 100yds (91m). Where it then bears right, take a gap stile by a gate in the left wall. A path leads away between wall and fence to a gate. Passing through, bear right uphill along the edge of a small plantation. Beyond a squeeze stile in the corner, head diagonally cross another small field. Keep beside the left hedge of the next field, the path levelling out as Castle Hill comes into view again and you meet a road.

4 Go right here, for just 20yds (18m), turning left through a kissing gate in the wall. Head away on a field-edge path, later slipping through a waymarked gap to continue, with the accompanying wall now on your right, towards a wood. Over a stile, keep to the edge of the next field, with a little wooded valley on your right. Leaving the wood behind and heading onwards to Lumb Head Farm, you can see Emley Moor mast to your right. Wind through the farmyard and join the access track to meet a road. Go right here, downhill. After a couple of cottages, pass through a gap stile in a wall on the right.

5 Walk down into the valley, following the wall on your right. Take a stile and a few stone steps to cross a meandering stream, Lumb Dike, on a plank bridge, at a delectable woodland spot. Climb away to a redundant stile and then turn left to follow the river, but at a higher level, through Molly Carr Wood. Descend to where two streams meet and accompany the combined watercourse along the valley bottom. After crossing a side beck walk on, rising to join a grass track that leads to a gate. However, bypass the gate and continue to a stone stile just beyond. Over that, bear left on a rough track passing behind a farmhouse. It leads around to the far end of the yard, from which a track takes you out to the road.

6 Go right, uphill; 75yds (69m) past a left-hand bend in the road, take a waymarked track sharply to the right, signed to Farnley Bank. Pass a house and when the track drops right to Farnley Bank Farm, take a stile ahead, and follow a field path uphill. Meet a road, and walk right, uphill, with good valley views, back into Farnley Tyas. At a T-junction, by the Golden Cock pub, turn right, then fork left by the church on to Butts Road to return to your car.

WHERE TO EAT AND DRINK Offering three real ales and an interesting menu, the Golden Cock in Farnley Tyas makes a perfect spot at which to finish the day.

The view from Castle Hill

DISTANCE 5.5 miles (8.8km)   MINIMUM TIME 2hrs 15min

ASCENT/GRADIENT 1,115ft (340m) ▲▲▲   LEVEL OF DIFFICULTY ✦✦✦

SEE MAP AND INFORMATION PANEL FOR WALK 18

Castle Hill is to the borough of Kirklees what Stoodley Pike is to Calderdale: a ubiquitous and much-loved landmark, visible for miles around. After the Norman castle was abandoned, during the 14th century, Castle Hill became a beacon site, one of a chain to warn of the Spanish Armada. During the 18th and 19th centuries Castle Hill was used for cock fighting, bull baiting and bare-knuckle fighting. Crowds gathered here for political rallies and religious meetings. The building that can be seen today is a relatively modern addition to this historic site, a Jubilee Tower built in 1898 to commemorate 60 years of Queen Victoria's reign. The grand tower rises 106ft (32m) above the hill's plateau, and dominates the skyline. It is open during summer weekends and school holidays, when you can climb the 165 steps inside and enjoy the spectacular panoramic views from the top. In the early 19th century, a tavern was built on the hill and later replaced with a larger hotel, but that too was demolished in 2005.

From Point **A** walk up the road to the crest of the hill, there turning sharply right on a lane signed to a car park, which takes you up to the plateau of Castle Hill. Having stopped to admire the view (expansive to every point of the compass), the tower and the earthworks, follow a path along the ramparts northeast from the tower. At the second dip, where it curves right, drop out left onto a descending flagged path. After 50yds (46m), where it swings left, carry on ahead beside a fence. Continue through kissing gates and then along a track to a junction by Clough Hall. Go right and immediately left through another kissing gate and walk on at the edge of a succession of fields before finally emerging onto a lane.

Go right down the hill past Wheatroyd Lodge. Then, approaching gates to another house, Wheatroyd Barn, turn off through a gap stile in the left fence. A winding path drops through trees, opening into a field at the bottom. Head across to another gap stile lower down the left boundary and follow a drive out to Lumb Lane. Go left to a junction and then right along Sharp Lane to reach Point **B** at the entrance to Royd House Farm.

Bretton Hall &
Country Park

DISTANCE 3 miles (4.8km)　　MINIMUM TIME 1hr 15min

ASCENT/GRADIENT 279ft (85m) ▲▲▲　　LEVEL OF DIFFICULTY ✚✚✚

PATHS Good paths and tracks all the way

LANDSCAPE Pasture, fields and parkland

SUGGESTED MAP OS Explorer 278 Sheffield & Barnsley

START/FINISH Grid reference: SE294125

DOG FRIENDLINESS Keep on lead in Country Park, but not allowed in buildings, Menagerie Wood (see Waypoint ❸) or around Upper Lake

PARKING Pay-and-display car park at Bretton Country Park, beside A637 near M1 junction 38

PUBLIC TOILETS At car park and the Sculpture Park

For more than half a millennium the Bretton estate had been held by just three families, the Dronsfields, Wentworths and Beaumonts, passing from one to the next by marriage. It was Sir William Wentworth who demolished the medieval hall and chapel in 1720 to make way for a fine new mansion in the grand Palladian style, a design inspired by memories of the classical cities of Europe visited during his Grand Tour. He sited his house on the hillside to take advantage of the views across the valley of the River Dearne and his son Sir Thomas continued his vision by landscaping the park and creating the lakes, which remain outstanding features of the estate.

A CENTRE OF EXCELLENCE FOR ARTS EDUCATION

The long line of tenure finally came to an end when it was sold to West Riding County Council after the war in 1947. In 1949, the Council founded a college for Arts and Education, which became renowned for its courses and subsequently affiliated with the University of Leeds. By the time the college closed in 2007, the Yorkshire Sculpture Park was already firmly established, continuing the ethos of education in supporting emerging artists and opening the estate and appreciation of art to a wider public.

THE SCULPTURE PARK

It may seem odd at first to find an outdoor sculpture park with an international reputation here in down-to-earth, rural West Yorkshire. But with world-renown sculptors Henry Moore coming from Castleford, and Dame Barbara Hepworth from Wakefield, perhaps it is not so strange after all.

The sculpture park was established in 1977, which made it the first such venture in the United Kingdom. Exhibitions of modern and contemporary art are displayed in over 200 acres (81ha) of parkland and four galleries, providing exhibitions, displays and projects. Over 200,000 people a year visit this extraordinary 'art gallery without walls'.

In the adjacent Bretton Country Park is a collection of sculptures by Henry Moore. He was one of the first sculptors to create works for siting in informal landscape settings where they would be encountered by people who might not otherwise visit a gallery. So it seems fitting that a dozen of Moore's monumental bronze figures have found a permanent home here. Both the Yorkshire Sculpture Park and Bretton Country Park are open all year round and entrance is free.

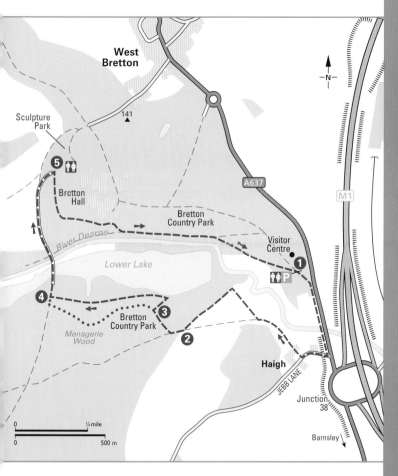

1 Rejoin the main road and walk right for 200yds (182m) before going right again into Jebb Lane. Follow it past cottages and around a bend, shortly turning off just before a barn on the right onto a track signed to Bretton Park. Go through a kissing gate at the end and head out across a field, closing with a wood on the left. Beyond the trees, cross a stile by a gate and continue along the other flank of the fence towards some more trees. Swing within the field corner and climb beside the boundary to reach an opening into the Bretton Park estate.

2 Bear right through a gap in the wall to a fork in the path. Take the right branch, signed as a footpath, which descends gently into woodland. Breaking cover, fork right and continue down to a second junction. Ignore the path off left, but at a fork a few paces further on, keep right into more trees and another junction.

3 Those with dogs must go left on a path skirting the perimeter of Menagerie Wood. At the far end pass through a field gate and walk forward to a track. Turn right through wrought iron gates into the park.

Without a dog you can take the right path, which, after crossing a ha-ha, winds through trees to a junction by the lake. Turn left through a gate and continue through the woods, where highland cattle freely roam. There are occasional views across the lake to Bretton Hall. The track runs beyond

the lake, leaving through a gate. Turn right along the main drive away from the wrought iron gates.

4 Follow the drive over two bridges to more wrought iron gates, passing through to continue gently uphill outside the perimeter fence. Keep ahead as a path joins from the left, but at a fork just beyond, bear right beside a field gate and continue up to emerge at the edge of a car park. The cafe at YSP Learning is just ahead, but the main complex lies a little further on.

5 There are any number of routes you might take through the Sculpture Park to explore the art, one being a bowered path that drops from the bottom of the car park, near the point at which you first entered. Meeting a crossing path, go left towards the hall. At the next junction, swing right towards the river and lake. However, just before reaching a bridge turn left through a gate to parallel the river at the edge of the open park. Through another gate, keep ahead past the foot of the lake and through more parkland. Eventually joining a drive, follow it right back to the car park.

WHERE TO EAT AND DRINK A licensed restaurant, cafe and coffee shops in the Sculpture Park offer the chance for a sit down, a light snack and leisurely reflections of the artworks on display throughout the park. If you're seeking pub food, try the Black Bull at Midgley, between West Bretton and Flockton. It's one of the Great British Carvery pubs, has a cosy atmosphere and serves meals all day.

WHILE YOU'RE THERE Take a trip to the National Coal Mining Museum for England, on the A642 halfway between Wakefield and Huddersfield. When the coal seams at the Caphouse Colliery were exhausted, during the mid-1980s, the site was converted into a museum. Visitors can explore the oldest coal mine shaft still in everyday use in Britain today, and learn about an industry which already seems to belong to our nation's past. Local miners are now guides through the workings, taking you 450ft (137m) below ground. There are also pit ponies, rides on the miners' train and a licensed cafe and shop.

Holmfirth and the Holme Valley

DISTANCE 4.5 miles (7.2km)	MINIMUM TIME 2hrs 30min
ASCENT/GRADIENT 558ft (170m) ▲▲▲	LEVEL OF DIFFICULTY ✦✦✦

PATHS Good paths and tracks, several stiles

LANDSCAPE Upland pasture

SUGGESTED MAP OS Explorer 288 Bradford & Huddersfield

START/FINISH Grid reference: SE143084

DOG FRIENDLINESS On lead in fields with livestock, off lead on lanes

PARKING Centre of Holmfirth gets very crowded, so park in Crown Bottom car park on Huddersfield Road

PUBLIC TOILETS Holmfirth

Holmfirth and the Holme Valley have been popularised as 'Summer Wine Country', forever linked to the whimsical TV series *Last of the Summer Wine,* written by Roy Clarke and starring a trio of incorrigible old buffers Compo, Foggy and Clegg.

The cast have become familiar faces around Holmfirth. So much so that when Londoner Bill Owen (loveable rogue 'Compo') died in 1999 at the age of 85, he was laid to rest overlooking the little town he had grown to call home.

Visitors come to Holmfirth in their droves, in search of film locations such as Sid's Café and Nora Batty's house. But Holmfirth takes its TV fame in its stride, for this isn't the first time that the town has starred in front of the cameras. In fact, Holmfirth very nearly became another Hollywood. Bamforths – better known for its naughty seaside postcards – began to make short films here in the early years of the last century. They were exported around the world to popular demand. Local people were drafted in as extras in Bamforths' overwrought dramas. Film production came to an end at the outbreak of World War I and, sadly, was never resumed.

HOLMFIRTH

Holmfirth town, much more than just a film set, is the real star – along with the fine South Pennine scenery which surrounds it. By the time you have completed half of this walk, you are a mile (1.6km) from the Peak District National Park.

The town grew rapidly with the textile trades, creating a tight-knit community in the valley bottom: a maze of ginnels, alleyways and narrow lanes. The River Holme, which runs through its middle, has flooded on many occasions. But the most devastating flood occurred back in 1852 when, after heavy rain, Bilberry Reservoir burst its banks. The resulting torrent of water destroyed the centre of Holmfirth and claimed 81 lives. The tragedy was reported at length on the front page of the London Illustrated News, complete with an artist's impression of the devastation. A public subscription fund was started to help the flood survivors to rebuild the town. These traumatic events are marked by a monument situated near the bus station.

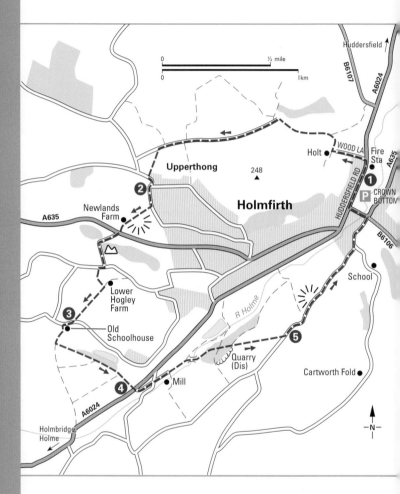

❶ From Crown Bottom car park, walk to the right along Huddersfield Road for just 100yds (91m) before bearing left opposite the fire station, up Wood Lane. The road soon narrows to a steep track. Keep left of a house and through a gate, to continue on a walled path. At the top of the hill, by a bench, follow the track to the right. Follow this track, soon enclosed, as it wheels left, down into a valley. Soon after you approach woodland, you have a choice of tracks: keep left on the walled path, uphill. Eventually join a stone farm track and after about 50yds (46m), cross the stile on the left, across a field path over steps and through a gate on the left to emerge by Midgeley Cottage. Turn left and follow the road as it bends through the top of the village.

2 Continue along the road, which wheels round to the right. Walk downhill, with great views opening up of the Holme Valley. After 150yds (137m) on the road, take a cinder track on the right. Walk down to meet a road. Cross over and take the lane ahead, steeply down into a little valley and up the other side. When this minor road forks at the top, go right, uphill. Immediately after the first house, go left, on a gravel track. Follow this track to Lower Hogley Farm where you keep right, past a knot of houses, to a gate and stile on to a field path, with a wall to your left. Go through four fields, aiming for the mast on the horizon, and descend to the road.

3 Go right for just 50yds (46m) to bear left around a path. Follow the walled footpath downhill, through a gate; as the footpath opens out into a grassy area, bear left on a grassy track down into the valley. Go through a gate and turn left, following the path down to a stile, on to an enclosed path. On approaching houses, take a stile and join a metalled track at a fork. Bear right here, then immediately left, on a narrow footpath between houses. Follow a field path through a gate; pass houses and a mill down to meet the main A6024 road.

4 Cross the road then, by a row of diminutive cottages, take Old Road to the left. Keep straight ahead when you reach a junction, down Water Street. Beyond a mill, cross the River Holme on a metal footbridge and follow a riverside path. The path opens into a field and soon forks right over duckboards. Keep to the right, uphill, and cross a stile to enter woodland. Continue in the same direction, following the uphill fork to the right until you reach some steps to the right. Go down the steps and turn right and immediately left, continuing in the same direction (uphill) to emerge at a field. Cross two fields and join a track by a house. Pass some more cottages to meet a road.

5 Go left, along the road. Enjoy fine views down into the Holme Valley, as you make the long descent back to Holmfirth.

WHERE TO EAT AND DRINK With so many visitors, Holmfirth is well supplied with pubs and tea shops, where you can stop for refreshments. Sid's Café and The Wrinkled Stocking Tea Room (next to Nora Batty's steps) will already be familiar to fans of *Last of the Summer Wine*.

WHAT TO SEE Holmfirth seems to have grown without much help from town planners. It is an intriguing maze of ginnels, stone steps and small cobbled alleyways, rising up between gritstone houses. After a few minutes' climb you will be rewarded with a view over the roofscape of the town.

WHILE YOU'RE THERE If you drive through Holmfirth on the A6024, you pass Holmbridge, then Holme, before the Holme Valley comes to a dramatic end, surrounded by a huge sweep of rugged moorland and splendid views. As you climb steeply to the height of Holme Moss, topped with a television mast, you enter the Peak District National Park.

From Addingham to Ilkley

DISTANCE 5.5 miles (8.8km)	MINIMUM TIME 2hrs
ASCENT/GRADIENT 360ft (110m) ▲▲▲	LEVEL OF DIFFICULTY ✚✚✚

PATHS Riverside path and field paths, some road walking

LANDSCAPE Rolling country and the River Wharfe

SUGGESTED MAP OS Explorer 297 Lower Wharfedale

START/FINISH Grid reference: SE083498

DOG FRIENDLINESS Keep on lead on minor roads and near livestock

PARKING Lay-by at eastern end of Addingham, on bend where North Street becomes Bark Lane by information panel

PUBLIC TOILETS Ilkley

Addingham extends for a mile (1.6km) on either side of the main street, with St Peter's Church at the eastern end of the village, close to the river, and is actually an amalgamation of three separate communities that grew as the textile trades expanded. Having been by-passed in recent years, Addingham is now a quiet backwater.

Within 50 years, from the end of the 17th century, Addingham's population quadrupled, from 500 to 2,000. Even here, at the gateway to the Yorkshire Dales, the textile industries flourished. At the height of the boom, there were six woollen mills in the village including Low Mill, built in 1787. The mill itself was demolished in 1972, but more houses were added to the mill-hands' cottages to create Low Mill Village, a pleasant riverside community.

ILKLEY

Ilkley seems to have more in common with Harrogate, its neighbour to the north, than with the textile towns of West Yorkshire. The Romans established an important fort here – believed to be *Olicana* – on a site close to where the parish church is today. Two Roman altars were incorporated into the base of the church tower, and taken into the church for safekeeping are three Anglo Saxon crosses that date to some time between the 8th or 9th century. One of the few tangible remains of the Roman settlement is a short stretch of wall near the handsome Manor House, which is now a museum.

Like nearby Harrogate, Ilkley's commercial fortunes changed dramatically with the discovery of medicinal springs. During the reign of Queen Victoria, the great and the good would come here to 'take the waters' and socialise at the town's hydros and hotels. Visitor numbers increased more with the coming of the railway. With its open-air swimming pool and riverside promenades, Ilkley was then almost an inland resort. It remains a prosperous and popular town today.

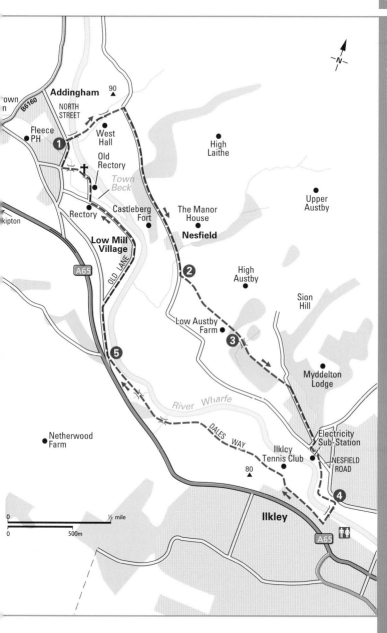

① Walk 50yds (46m) up the road, and take stone steps down to the right, (signed 'Dales Way'). Turn immediately right again, dropping to cross the River Wharfe on a suspension bridge. Follow a metalled path along a field edge. Turn over a stream at the end and follow a farm track left to emerge on the bend of a minor road. Go right here; after about 0.5 miles (800m) of road walking you reach the little community of Nesfield.

② About 100yds (91m) beyond the last house, and immediately after the road crosses a stream, bear left up a stony track (signed as a footpath to High Austby). Immediately take a stile between two gates. Cross to the gate in the far-right corner. Through it, there is no obvious path, but follow the boundary on your right, heading towards Low Austby Farm. Carry on in the final field past the farm, bearing slightly left beneath a gnarled oak towards the wood ahead.

3 Cross a footbridge over a stream; beyond a stile you enter woodland. Follow a path downhill, leaving the wood by another step stile. Bear right across the slope of a field to a stile at the far end, to enter more woodland. Follow an obvious path through the trees, before reaching a road via a wall stile. Go right, downhill, to reach a road junction. Go right again, cross Nesfield Road, and take a path to the left of an electricity sub-station. Leading to the river, it accompanies the wooded bank to Ilkley's old stone bridge. Cross to the south side.

4 To explore the town, go left by the river through the park. Swing right towards its far end to come out by the ancient church. Otherwise, follow the Dales Way back to Addingham by turning right on a riverside path. At

its end, keep ahead along the drive to Ilkley Tennis Club. Reaching the clubhouse, bear off left through a kissing gate across pasture. Part-way along the second field, take a kissing gate on the left and walk beside two more fields back to the river. Over a stream, continue through trees. Beyond a second stream, a stony path drops back down to the Wharfe. Carry on at the edge of grazing, emerging at the far end onto a now-quiet lane, once the main Skipton road.

5 Walk right for just over 0.25 miles (400m) before turning off along Old Lane. Reaching Low Mill village, bear right to follow the street between cottages. At the end, keep ahead on a path that quickly reverts to a lane. After another 0.25 miles (400m), beyond the old Rectory set back within spacious grounds, look for a gate on the right from which steps drop to a tiny arched bridge over Town Beck. Swing left across a pasture in front of the church to join a drive at the far side. Go left but immediately bear off right through a gate over another bridge. Wind between cottages to emerge onto North Road and turn right back to the parking spot.

WHERE TO EAT AND DRINK In Addingham try the Crown Inn or the Fleece for traditional pub food. At the bottom end of Ilkley you are close to the 'The Taps' or the Ilkley Moor Vaults as it officially called, and the Riverside Hotel, which is particularly child-friendly.

WHILE YOU'RE THERE Addingham lies at the northwestern edge of the county. Just a mile (1.6km) to the north you enter the Yorkshire Dales National Park. By following the B6160 you soon come to Bolton Abbey, with its priory ruins in an idyllic setting by a bend in the River Wharfe.

Right: The old, stone packhorse bridge in Ilkley (Walk 22)

Shipley Glen Tramway and Baildon Moor

DISTANCE 4 miles (6.4km)	MINIMUM TIME 1hr 30min

ASCENT/GRADIENT 640ft (195m) ▲▲▲   LEVEL OF DIFFICULTY ✚✚✚

PATHS Moor and field paths, no stiles

LANDSCAPE Moorland, fields and gritstone rocks

SUGGESTED MAP OS Explorer 288 Bradford & Huddersfield

START/FINISH Grid reference: SE131389

DOG FRIENDLINESS Keep on lead by roads or near livestock

PARKING Lay-bys on Glen Road, between Bracken Hall Countryside Centre and Old Glen House pub

PUBLIC TOILETS At Bracken Hall Countryside Centre; also in Saltaire

For the people of Shipley and Saltaire, Baildon Moor has traditionally represented a taste of the countryside on their doorsteps. Mill-hands could leave the mills and cramped terraced streets behind, and breathe clean Pennine air. They could listen to the song of the skylark and the bubbling cry of the curlew. There were heather moors to tramp across, gritstone rocks to scramble up and, at Shipley Glen, springy sheep-grazed turf on which to spread out a picnic blanket. There was also once a funfair to visit – not a small affair either but a veritable theme park.

Towards the end of the 19th century Shipley Glen was owned by a Colonel Maude, who created a number of attractions. Visitors could enjoy the sundry delights of the Switchback Railway, Marsden's Menagerie, the Horse Tramway and the Aerial Runway. More sedate pleasures could be found at the Camera Obscura, the boating lake in the Japanese garden, and the Temperance Tea Room and Coffee House.

Sam Wilson, a local entrepreneur, played his own part in developing Shipley Glen. In 1895 he created the Shipley Glen Tramway. Saltaire people could now stroll through Roberts Park, past the steely-gazed statue of Sir Titus Salt, and enjoy the tram-ride to the top of the glen. Thousands of people would clamber, each weekend, on to the little cable-hauled 'toastrack' cars. As one car went up the hill, another would descend on an adjacent track.

In commercial terms, the heyday of Shipley Glen was during the Edwardian era. On busy days, as many as 17,000 people would take the tramway up to the pleasure gardens. Losing out to more sophisticated entertainments, however, Shipley Glen went into a slow decline. Sadly, all the attractions are now gone, but you can still take the ride on the tramway – which runs on Sunday afternoons throughout the year (weather permitting). There is an attractive souvenir shop at the top, while the bottom station houses a small museum and replica Edwardian shop.

The Old Glen House is still a popular pub, though the former Temperance Tea Room and Coffee House have been transformed into the Bracken Hall Countryside Centre. Local people still enjoy the freedom of the heather moorland. Despite all the changes, Shipley Glen retains a stubbornly old-fashioned air, and is all the better for it.

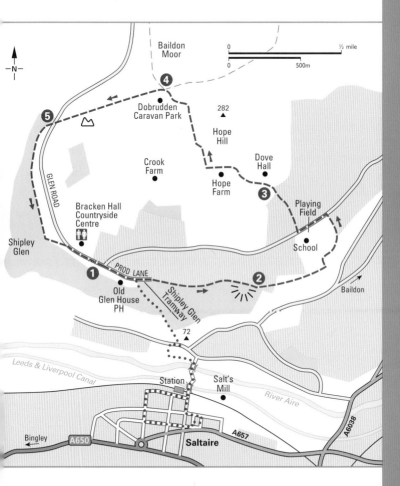

❶ Walk down Glen Road, passing the Old Glen House pub. Continue as the road becomes Prod Lane, signed as a cul-de-sac. Where the road ends at the entrance to the Shipley Glen Tramway, keep straight ahead to locate an enclosed path to the right of a house. Follow this path, with houses on your left, and woodland

to your right. As you come to a metal barrier, ignore a path to the left. Keep straight on downhill. 100yds (91m) beyond the barrier, there is a choice of paths; bear left here, contouring the steep hillside and soon getting good views over Saltaire, Shipley and the Aire Valley.

2 Keep going as a path later joins from the right, undulating through scrub and more open heath beneath the old quarried face of a sandstone cliff. After a further 0.25 miles (400m), watch for a stepped path and handrail climbing to the left. At the top, turn right on a fenced path that skirts two sides of a school playing field. Emerging onto a road, cross and go left for 150yds (138m). Drawing level with the entrance to the primary school, turn off onto a narrow, enclosed path that climbs between the houses on the right. Meeting a street higher up, cross to the ongoing path. Continue up to a gate, which opens out onto the bottom of a sloping pasture.

3 Go half left uphill to a kissing gate at the far corner of the field. Head out to join an access track along the field top to Hope Farm. Walk past the buildings on a cinder track, leaving just before its end onto a bridleway through a gate on the right. Emerging onto Baildon Moor, the onward path runs alongside the wall on the left. Keep straight on beyond the corner towards a caravan park. Cross a metalled track leading to the camp site and keep ahead to the corner of the boundary wall. Swing left to walk on beside it.

4 Walk gradually downhill towards the distant suburbs of Bingley. When the wall bears left, keep straight ahead, through bracken, more steeply downhill. Cross a metalled track and continue on down to meet Glen Road once again.

5 Follow the path along the rocky edge of wooded Shipley Glen, which will eventually lead you back to the Bracken Hall Countryside Centre and your car.

WHERE TO EAT AND DRINK Sir Titus Salt wouldn't allow public houses in Saltaire, but that prohibition didn't extend to Shipley Glen, where the Old Glen House, near the upper tramway station, is open for lunches and evening meals from Tuesday to Saturday and lunch on Sunday. The food is locally sourced wherever possible with fresh herbs coming from the garden, and they boast that nothing is frozen except the home-made ice cream. You'll find local beers on tap too, such as Saltaire Blonde and Timothy Taylor's Landlord.

WHAT TO SEE Call in at the Bracken Hall Countryside Centre on Glen Road, which has a number of interesting displays about the history of Shipley Glen, its flora and its fauna. There are also temporary exhibitions on particular themes, interactive features and a programme of children's activities throughout the year. The gift shop sells maps, guides, natural history books and ice creams.

WHILE YOU'RE THERE Be sure to visit Salts Mill, a giant of a building on a truly epic scale. At the height of production 3,000 people worked here. There were 1,200 looms clattering away, weaving as much as 30,000 yards of cloth every working day. The mill is a little quieter these days – with a permanent exhibition of artworks by David Hockney, another of Bradford's most famous sons.

Shipley Glen and Saltaire

DISTANCE 2.5 miles (4km)   MINIMUM TIME 1hr 30min

ASCENT/GRADIENT 328ft (100m) ▲▲▲   LEVEL OF DIFFICULTY ✚✚✚

SEE MAP AND INFORMATION PANEL FOR WALK 23

There's so much to see in Shipley Glen and Saltaire. Stroll out on Walk 23 in the morning, have lunch at the Old Glen House, then take the tramway down into the valley and explore Salt's Mill and the model village of Saltaire.

From the Old Glen House walk back down Glen Road to the upper terminus of the Shipley Glen Tramway and take the easy way down into the valley (or, if the tramway is not running, follow the adjacent path). At the bottom of the hill is a small museum devoted to the chequered history of the tramway. Continue down the path and out to the main road. Go right and then left into Roberts Park, where a statue of Sir Titus Salt still stands. At the bottom-left corner of the park a footbridge spans the River Aire. After swinging left and right across the Leeds and Liverpool Canal, the Saltaire Mill is then on your left. Carry on over the railway line to reach the town. After a leisurely exploration of Titus Salt's model village, retrace your steps – and take the tramway – back up to Shipley Glen.

Saltaire's founding father was Sir Titus Salt, a Victorian industrialist and patriarch, who owned textile mills in Bradford. He made a fortune from spinning alpaca fleece and, seeing the smoky, Dickensian squalor of life in the city, decided to build a new settlement for his employees.

Sir Titus designed Saltaire as a community where his mill workers could live in clean, sanitary conditions. Begun in 1851, it was 20 years in the making. As a contrast to many areas of Bradford, even the most modest dwelling in Saltaire had gas, running water and a toilet. In his plan Sir Titus included schools, a bathhouse, laundry, hospital and a row of almshouses. A workers' dining room could seat 800. The neat streets of terraced houses were named after the founder (Titus Street), his wife, Caroline, and children... not forgetting the reigning monarch (Victoria Street) and her consort (Albert Road).

The centrepiece of his scheme was Salt's Mill, a monumental example of industrial architecture which straddles the Leeds and Liverpool Canal. The chimney is a copy of the bell tower of a church in Venice. In recent years the mill has enjoyed a new lease of life as a showcase for the artworks of David Hockney, who was born in Bradford.

Surprise View and Otley Chevin

DISTANCE 3.5 miles (5.7km)	MINIMUM TIME 1hr 30min	
ASCENT/GRADIENT 525ft (160m) ▲▲▲	LEVEL OF DIFFICULTY ✦✦✦	

PATHS Easy walking on good paths and forestry tracks, no stiles

LANDSCAPE Heath and woodland

SUGGESTED MAP OS Explorer 297 Lower Wharfedale

START/FINISH Grid reference: SE204441

DOG FRIENDLINESS Dogs can run free all over the Chevin

PARKING Beacon House car park on Yorkgate, opposite The Royalty Inn

PUBLIC TOILETS None on route

This walk begins at Surprise View and, if this is your first visit, you will have a surprise indeed. By strolling just a few paces from your car you can enjoy a breathtaking panorama across Lower Wharfedale. Almscliffe Crag is a prominent landmark in the valley and, on a clear day, you may be able to see Simon's Seat and even the famous White Horse carved into the hillside at Kilburn, some 30 miles (48km) away. With so much to see, it is easy to forget that you are only a mile (1.6km) away from the bustle of the Leeds–Bradford International Airport.

CHEVIN FOREST PARK

The Chevin has traditionally been a popular destination for walkers and picnickers. In 1944 Major Fawkes of Farnley Hall gave a piece of land on the Chevin to the people of Otley. By 1989, when it was designated a local nature reserve, the Chevin Forest Park had grown to 700 acres (283ha) of woodland, heath and gritstone crags.

Local people come here to walk their dogs and the broad forest tracks are ideal for horse riders and mountain bikers. The park is criss-crossed by any number of good waymarked paths and the walk featured here is merely one possibility.

OTLEY

The market town of Otley, which straddles the River Wharfe and is well worth visiting in its own right. Thomas Chippendale, the famous furniture maker, was born in Otley in 1710 and it was here that the Wharfedale Printing Machine was developed, the first major breakthrough since the invention of the printing press in the 15th century.

Left: Looking across the weir towards Salt's Mill in Saltaire (Walk 24)

Otley was granted its market charter by Henry III back in 1222, and the cobbled market square still occupies the centre of town. On market days (Tuesdays, Fridays and Saturdays) the stalls overflow along the main street of Kirkgate. There are weekly livestock markets and a monthly farmers' market too and Otley Show is a big date in the local calendar each spring.

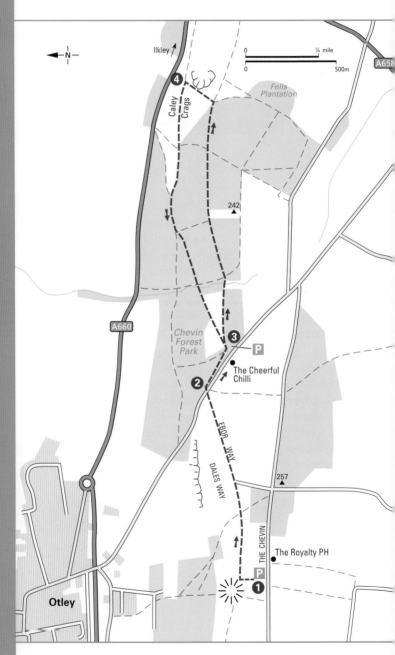

Ilkley

Fells Plantation

Caley Crags

A658

242

A660

Chevin Forest Park

The Cheerful Chilli

EBOR WAY

DALES WAY

257

THE CHEVIN

The Royalty PH

Otley

The Otley Folk Festival attracts music lovers every autumn when, over a long weekend, you can hardly move for mummers and morris dancers. For outdoor relaxation, Wharfemeadows Park offers riverside strolls, gardens and a children's play area.

❶ Walk through the car park to find a path running along the ridge overlooking the valley. Follow it right and keep to the higher branch at a fork. Beyond a gate, ignore the trail off right and continue ahead on the descending track that leads to the main road.

❷ Cross to a signed footpath into the trees opposite, which runs parallel to the road, to a junction of paths below a small car park.

❸ There, turn left along the middle path, a broad, tree-lined avenue signed as the Dales Way Link. Keep ahead, shortly crossing a bridge. Climb away, still keeping to the main trail. Eventually, at a junction of paths at the far end of the plantation, go through a kissing gate on the left. Take the rightmost of the two paths leading away, keeping ahead to meet another path running along the rim of the rocky edge that overlooks the valley below.

❹ After admiring the view, follow the path left, joining with other paths to reach a kissing gate. Pass through and keep ahead on a broader track, the Ebor Way, which leads past the foundation remains of Keeper's Cottage. The undulating path runs for 0.5 miles (800m) through the forest to reach a bridge. Wind left and right as you climb away, shortly returning to the junction of paths at the corner of the car park. Turn right and reverse your outward route back to the car park on top of The Chevin.

WHERE TO EAT AND DRINK The Royalty on top of the Chevin was a popular walkers' pub, but at the time of revision, had closed down. There are hopes it might re-open, but in the meantime, The Cheerful Chilli tearoom by the car park on East Chevin Road and the many pubs, chip and tea shops down in Otley offer alternatives.

WHAT TO SEE Otley Chevin is a favourite place for enthusiasts of radio-controlled gliders to fly their aircraft. The shape of the hill creates a series of thermals which give uplift, allowing the fliers to perform aerobatic manoeuvres without the irritating buzz of little motors.

WHILE YOU'RE THERE Visit Otley, a characterful little market town by the River Wharfe. The little nooks and corners are well worth investigating. In the churchyard you will find an elaborate memorial to the 23 workers who were killed during the construction of the nearby Bramhope railway tunnel between 1845–49.

Overleaf: Chevin ridge on the south side of Wharfedale (Walk 25)

Halifax and the Shibden Valley

DISTANCE 5 miles (8km)   MINIMUM TIME 2hrs 15min

ASCENT/GRADIENT 1,148ft (350m) ▲▲▲   LEVEL OF DIFFICULTY ✦✦✦

PATHS Old packhorse tracks and field paths, no stiles

LANDSCAPE Surprisingly rural, considering the proximity to Halifax

SUGGESTED MAP OS Explorer 288 Bradford & Huddersfield

START/FINISH Grid reference: SE096251

DOG FRIENDLINESS Keep on lead crossing busy roads

PARKING Choice of pay-and-display car parks in Halifax

PUBLIC TOILETS Halifax bus station and Shibden Park

Set amongst the Pennine hills, Halifax was a town in the vanguard of the Industrial Revolution. Its splendid civic buildings and huge mills are an indication of the town's prosperity, won from the woollen trade. Ironically, the most splendid building of all came close to being demolished. The Piece Hall, built in 1779, predates the industrial era. Here, in a total of 315 rooms on three colonnaded floors, the hand weavers of the district would offer their wares (known as 'pieces') for sale to cloth merchants. The colonnades surround a massive square. This is a building that would not look out of place in Renaissance Italy.

The mechanisation of the weaving process left the Piece Hall largely redundant. In the intervening years it has served a variety of purposes, including as a venue for political oration and as a wholesale market. During the 1970s it was spruced up and given a new lease of life. It now houses a visitor centre, art gallery and speciality shops and hosts events throughout the year.

THE MAGNA VIA

The cobbled thoroughfare up Beacon Hill is known as the Magna Via. Until 1741, when a turnpike road was built, this was the only practicable approach to Halifax from the east, for both foot and packhorse traffic. Also known as Wakefield Gate, the Magna Via linked up with the Long Causeway, the old high level road to Burnley. That intrepid 18th-century traveller, Daniel Defoe, was one of those who struggled up this hill. 'We quitted Halifax not without some astonishment at its situation, being so surrounded with hills, and those so high as makes the coming in and going out of it exceedingly troublesome'. The route was superseded in the 1820s by the turnpike constructed through Godley Cutting. Today the Magna Via, too steep for modern motor vehicles, remains a fascinating relic of the past.

SHIBDEN HALL

Situated on a hill above Halifax, this magnificent half-timbered house is set in 90 acres (36ha) of beautiful, rolling parkland. Dating from 1420, the hall has been owned by prominent local families – the Oates, Saviles, Waterhouses and, latterly, the Listers. All these families left their mark on the fabric of the house, but the core of the original house remains intact. The rooms are furnished in period style, to show how they might have looked over almost six centuries. The oak furniture and panelling has that patina of age that antique forgers try in vain to emulate. Barns and other outbuildings have been converted into a folk museum, with displays of old vehicles, tools and farm machinery.

When Emily Brontë created Thrushcross Grange in her only novel *Wuthering Heights*, she may have had Shibden Hall in mind. It certainly proved a suitable location in 1991 for a film adaptation of the famous story, starring Ralph Fiennes as Heathcliffe and Juliette Binoche as Cathy.

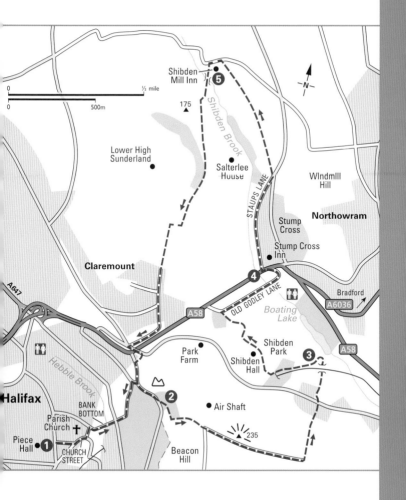

1 Begin opposite the tall spire that once belonged to Square Church, walking down Alfred Street East and left along Church Street, passing the smoke-blackened parish church. Bear left again into Lower Kirkgate, then right along Bank Bottom. Cross Hebble Brook and walk uphill; where the road bears sharp left, keep straight ahead up a steep cobbled lane, the Magna Via. Meeting a road at the top, go right for about 200yds (183m). Just after the entrance to a warehouse (Aquaspersion), take a cobbled path on the left that makes a steep ascent up Beacon Hill.

2 Keep with the main trail, which, higher up, curves left over the shoulder of the hill and runs beneath a high buttress wall to a kissing gate and barrier. Walk forward along a broad cinder track, taking the left fork a little further on where views open across the surprisingly rural Shibden Valley. After a further 100yds (91m), take a walled path on the left. Drop steeply to a small housing estate and turn right out to the main road. Almost opposite, beside a farm entrance, a path continues downhill, passing beneath the railway line into Shibden Park.

3 Walk forward to the lake and bear left past the boathouse up to a junction with the main drive. Go left and then left again in front of a pool onto a track that climbs beside the wooded railway embankment. Reaching another pool, the house and gardens are to the left, otherwise, branch right towards the car park. At the next junction, drop right past a display of traditional walling, descending through trees to a drive. Climb left to the park entrance and turn right down Old Godley Lane. It finally swings left up to the main road at Stump Cross.

4 Cross over the road and take Staups Lane, to the left of the Stump Cross Inn. Walk along the lane, which soon becomes cobbled, to meet another road at the top. Go left and immediately left again down a drive, which, through a gate, continues across the fields into Shibden Dale. Emerging at the far end on to a lane, turn left down to the Shibden Mill Inn.

5 Swing left past the pub, leaving the far end of the car park on a track across Shibden Beck. At a fork, bear right, later passing an isolated house. Beyond, a narrower path winds up to Claremount. Keep ahead along a street that ultimately bends right above Godley Cutting. At the end, go left over a bridge spanning the main road and then immediately descend steps on the right to a street below. Go left to its end and then right to retrace your outward route into Halifax.

WHERE TO EAT AND DRINK At the halfway point of this walk is Shibden Mill Inn. A sympathetic reworking of an old mill, this is the place for good food and, when the weather is kind, a drink in the beer garden.

WHILE YOU'RE THERE Children will enjoy a visit to visit Eureka!, the ultimate hands-on discovery museum, designed specifically for children up to the age of 12.

A circuit of Norland Moor

DISTANCE 5 miles (8km)	MINIMUM TIME 2hrs

ASCENT/GRADIENT 722ft (220m) ▲▲▲   LEVEL OF DIFFICULTY ✚✚✚

PATHS Good moorland paths and tracks

LANDSCAPE Heather moor and woodland

SUGGESTED MAP OS Explorer OL21 South Pennines

START/FINISH Grid reference: SE055218

DOG FRIENDLINESS Dogs can roam off lead, though watch for grazing sheep

PARKING Small public car park opposite Moorcock Inn, on unclassified road immediately south of Sowerby Bridge

PUBLIC TOILETS None on route

Norland Moor and North Dean Woods are close to the start of the Calderdale Way, a 50-mile (80km) circuit of the borough of Calderdale. There are panoramic views straight away, as the waymarked walk accompanies the edge of Norland Moor. The route was inaugurated during the 1970s to link some of the most impressive Pennine landscapes and historical sites – moors, mills, gritstone outcrops, wooded cloughs, weavers' hamlets and industrial towns – into an invigorating walk.

NORLAND MOOR

Norland Moor is a 253-acre (102ha) tract of heather moorland overlooking Sowerby Bridge and both the Calder and Ryburn valleys. Criss-crossed by paths, it is popular with local walkers; driven by old quarry workings, it is a reminder that here in West Yorkshire you are seldom far from a site of industry.

Ladstone Rock is a gritstone outcrop with a distinctive profile that stares out over the Ryburn Valley from the edge of Norland Moor. If you can believe the stories, barbaric human sacrifices were carried out on Ladstone Rock by blood-thirsty druids, and convicted witches were thrown off it. The name may derive from Celtic roots, meaning to cut or to kill.

There is a tradition in the South Pennines of carving inspirational quotations into such rocks. And here on Ladstone Rock, amongst the names, dates and expressions of undying love, is a small metal plaque inscribed with a short psalm from the Bible.

WAINHOUSE TOWER

As you leave the nature reserve of North Dean Woods behind, you get good views across the valley to Sowerby Bridge and the outskirts of Halifax. Dominating the view is a curious edifice known as Wainhouse Tower (and also tellingly, as Wainhouse Folly). It was built by John Wainhouse, who had inherited his uncle's dyeworks. His first plan was to build a tall chimney that would help to disperse the noxious fumes from the dyeworks. But then he decided to add a spiral staircase, inside the chimney, leading up to an ornate viewing platform at the top. The tower was finished in the 1870s and is open to the public on a few occasions each year. To climb to the full height of the tower, 253ft (77m), you need to tackle more than 400 steps.

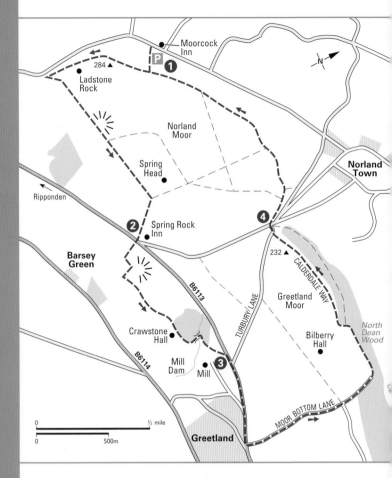

❶ Walk uphill opposite the Moorcock Inn, bearing successively right near the top to follow a clear path along the edge of Norland Moor. Enjoy expansive views across the Calder

Valley as you pass the gritstone outcrop known as Ladstone Rock. Keep straight ahead, now on a more substantial track which descends to run beside the road. Reaching the corner of a caravan site, turn left beside the wall. Ignore a waymarked gate and bear left with the path, climbing across the slope of the heath to meet another wall corner higher up. Continue by the wall for 0.5 miles (800m), ignoring a junction and ultimately meeting a farm track. Follow it right to emerge beside the Spring Rock Inn.

2 Cross the road and continue on the narrowest of walled paths opposite. Extensive views open up as the path later goes right, down stone steps. Where the walled path ends, go left on a track. Keep ahead past cottages and again further on, as a lane joins from the right. After 200yds (183m), bear right at a fork, branching off left just before the gates of a house along a waymarked path into a small wood. The path soon descends to cross a stream on a stone-slab bridge, then bears right uphill to meet a walled track. Cross to the ongoing path, which follows a wall behind houses before turning out between them to meet the B6113.

3 Walk right, along the road to the outskirts of Greetland and turn left into Moor Bottom Lane. Continue ahead along this straight track for 0.5 miles (800m). Entering North Dean Wood, the track curves left to a fork. Take a marked path between the two branches and follow a wall along the upper edge of the woodland. Over a stile, keep right at the edge of a large field above the wood. Eventually, a developing track leads out through a gate onto a lane. Go right, past its junction with Norland Road to a sharp right-hand bend.

4 Turn left on a stony track across Norland Moor. At a junction beside a pylon, bear left on a path following the line of overhead cables. Ignoring side paths, keep ahead, eventually joining a prominent path from the right along the edge. Shortly after passing a railed enclosure, bear off right by a marker post, dropping to the path by which you first ascended from the car park.

WHERE TO EAT AND DRINK Your best choice is the Moorcock Inn, opposite the car park. This is a popular meeting place for the local walking and rambling clubs – either before their walk on the moors or after.

WHAT TO SEE The plateau of Norland Moor, overlooking Sowerby Bridge and the Calder Valley, is a particular delight in late summer, when the heather is in purple flower. Although we now consider heather to be the natural plant to grow on these moors, its introduction is relatively recent. Heather will not grow in the shade, and so it was not until all the trees had been cleared off these hills by early settlers that it really took a hold. You should also look for the bittersweet-tasting bilberry, which is a favourite with grazing sheep around the end of June, and the less palatable (and mildly poisonous) crowberries, which cluster on rockier ground.

WHILE YOU'RE THERE Eclipsing the original hillside Norse settlement, Sowerby Bridge developed as the junction between two important waterways, the Rochdale Canal and the Calder and Hebble Navigation. Warehouses and mills grew around the basin, which, now restored as a marina, provides an attractive focus to the town. Immediately upstream on the Rochdale Canal is Tuel Lane Lock, which, with a fall of almost 20ft (6m) is the deepest in the country.

Bingley and the St Ives Estate

DISTANCE 6 miles (9.7km)	MINIMUM TIME 2hrs 30min

ASCENT/GRADIENT 853ft (260m) ▲▲▲   LEVEL OF DIFFICULTY ✛✛✛

PATHS Good paths and tracks throughout

LANDSCAPE Woodland, park and river

SUGGESTED MAP OS Explorer 288 Bradford & Huddersfield

START/FINISH Grid reference: SE107391

DOG FRIENDLINESS Can be off lead on St Ives Estate

PARKING Car parks in Bingley

PUBLIC TOILETS In Myrtle Place by the park

Sitting astride both the River Aire and the Leeds and Liverpool Canal, in a steep-sided valley, Bingley is a typical West Yorkshire town. With its locks, wharves and plethora of mills, the town grew in size and importance during the 19th century as the textile trades expanded. But Bingley's pre-eminence did not begin with the Industrial Revolution; it is, in fact, one of the county's oldest settlements, with its market charter being granted by King John as far back as 1212.

In keeping with its age, Bingley has a number of splendid old buildings including the Old White Horse, a venerable coaching inn, where King John is reputed to have stayed. Ancient and modern sit side-by-side in Bingley which, unfortunately, has more than its fair share of architectural monstrosities, dating from recent times.

Halliwell Sutcliffe, author of such books as *The Striding Dales* and *By Moor and Fell*, lived in Bingley while his father was headmaster of the town's Grammar School.

RIVER AIRE

The River Aire rises close to the village of Malham, in the limestone dales of North Yorkshire, and flows past Bingley. By the time it joins the Ouse and decants into the Humber Estuary, it has been one of the hardest worked watercourses in Yorkshire. When the textile trades were at their height, the Aire was both a source of power for the woollen mills and a convenient dumping ground for industrial waste. But, like so many other West Yorkshire rivers, the water quality is now greatly improved.

ST IVES

For part of this walk, you will be exploring the St Ives Estate, which from 1636 was owned by one of Bingley's most prominent families, the

Ferrands. It was William Ferrand who, during the 1850s, landscaped the estate and created many of the paths and tracks that climb steeply up through the woods. The view from the top of the hill is ample reward for your efforts. From the gritstone outcrop known – somewhat fancifully – as the Druid's Altar, you have a splendid panorama across Bingley and the Aire Valley.

There is an inscription on Lady Blantyre's Rock, passed later on this walk, which commemorates William Ferrand's mother-in-law. Lady Blantyre often used to sit in the shade of this rock and read a book. A splendid notion: a monument to idleness. Near by is an obelisk with a dedication to William Ferrand himself. St Ives, a little wooded oasis on Bingley's doorstep, is now looked after by Bradford council on behalf of local people.

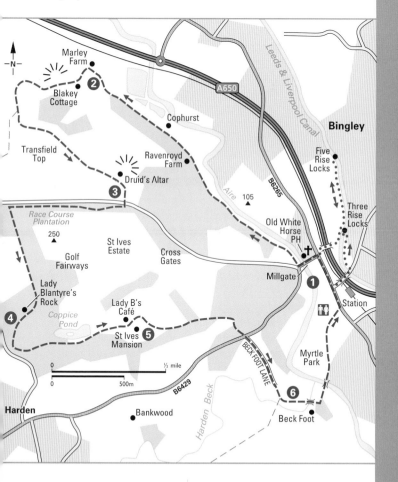

❶ Walk northwest from the centre of Bingley towards the church. Go left at the traffic lights beside the Old White Horse pub into Millgate. Cross the River Aire and take the first right, Ireland Street. Swing immediately right again and then left along a riverside track, soon leaving the town behind. Reaching Ravenroyd Farm, bear right and pass between farm buildings to continue on a walled track to Cophurst. Pass left of the cottage and continue beside a wood at the edge of successive pastures.

2 A developing track leaves the third pasture through a gap. Continue to a stile and gate and skirt a hillock, eventually leaving over a stile by Marley Farm. Follow the rough track up left, passing Marley Brow. Where the track subsequently swings into a farm, bear off right on a grass trail across a bracken and scrub slope, ultimately winding up to a small gate. A narrow path rises through more trees. Keep right and then left at successive forks, shortly joining a wall on the right bounding the top of the wood. Eventually, after crossing a broad track, the path leads to a rocky outcrop known as the Druid's Altar.

3 Bear right, after the rocks, to come to a meeting of tracks. Go through a gap in the wall opposite, on to a walled track into the St Ives Estate. Leave immediately through a kissing gate on the right on to a path that runs pleasantly for 0.5 miles (800m) within Race Course Plantation. Ignoring the kissing gate leading out at the end, go left, now descending, initially still within trees through a golf course and then at the edge of open heather moor. When the accompanying wall later turns away, bear right with the main path, dropping through wood once more to come upon Lady Blantyre's Rock.

4 Descend with the main path past exuberant displays of rhododendrons and on beside Coppice Pond. Meeting a metalled drive, bear left, soon passing Lady B's Café, the golf clubhouse and then, set back on the right, the house itself, St Ives Mansion.

5 Beyond the house, curve right and left to follow the main drive downhill for 0.5 miles (800m). Just after passing a car park, take a path left into woodland. Keep right where it immediately forks, to reach the B6429, the Bingley to Cullingworth road. Cross it and continue downhill on narrow Beck Foot Lane. After houses the lane becomes an unmade track leading down to a delectable spot: here you will find Beckfoot Farm, in a wooded setting by Harden Beck, with a ford and an old packhorse bridge that dates back to 1723.

6 Cross the bridge to Beckfoot Farm and bear left past allotments. Where they end, take a path left to a footbridge over the River Aire. Walk ahead through Myrtle Park, leaving at the far side behind the former Bradford and Bingley building. Go forward past the swimming pool and then right into the town.

WHERE TO EAT AND DRINK With 12th-century origins, the Old White Horse Inn is Bingley's oldest pub and housed the court, police cells and gibbet. Serving food at weekends, it has oodles of character, and claims several resident ghosts. At St Ives, try Lady B's Café, which is licensed and offers hot and cold snacks all day.

WHAT TO SEE Having been removed from the main street, Bingley's ancient stocks, butter cross and old market hall were re-sited in front of the Bingley Arts Centre, near the Ferrands Arms.

Bingley and the Five Rise Locks

DISTANCE 1.5 miles (2.4km)   MINIMUM TIME 30min

ASCENT/GRADIENT 131ft (40m) ▲▲▲   LEVEL OF DIFFICULTY ✚✚✚

SEE MAP AND INFORMATION PANEL FOR WALK 28

Walkers with an interest in canal history may want to extend Walk 28 to include a visit to Bingley's famous 'staircase' of locks which, after the Damart factory (makers of thermal underwear), is Bingley's best-known landmark. The Leeds and Liverpool Canal is, at 127 miles (205km), the longest canal in Britain. It was the first of the three trans-Pennine canals to be started, in 1770, and the last to be finished, in 1816. Unlike many of the other watercourses built during the years of 'canal mania', the Leeds and Liverpool proved to be profitable almost immediately.

The canal achieved its stated principal aim – giving easier access to overseas markets through the port of Liverpool for the mill owners of West Yorkshire. It cut the costs of transport in the heartlands of the textile industry, helping to bring considerable prosperity to towns like Bingley, Shipley and Keighley, that were largely dependent on the wool trade.

Leave the main street opposite Barclays Bank along Park Road. Cross a long bridge spanning the railway, bypass and canal and then immediately leave left down to a canalside path. Walk away, rounding a bend behind the Damart factory to find the Three Rise Locks. Cross the canal on one of the bridges and continue upstream on the opposite bank to the Five Rise Locks, 0.5 miles (800m) further on.

To cope with the undulating topography of the trans-Pennine route, there are 91 locks on the Leeds and Liverpool Canal, of which no fewer than eight can be found on this short stretch of the canal at Bingley. In a remarkable feat of engineering, the rise of five locks lifts the level of the canal about 66ft (20m) in a space of just 100yds (91m). It can take some time for narrowboats to negotiate this picturesque bottleneck, but, after all, if people are in a hurry they tend to pick another mode of transport.

Return along the tow path to the Three-Rise Locks and turn right across a footbridge that spans the bypass and railway line. It leads back to the main road near the parish church.

The River Aire and the Leeds and Liverpool Canal

DISTANCE 3.5 miles (5.7km)	MINIMUM TIME 1hr 15min

ASCENT/GRADIENT 230ft (70m) ▲▲▲   LEVEL OF DIFFICULTY +++

PATHS Riverside path and canal tow path, no stiles

LANDSCAPE Surprisingly rural, considering you are so close to Leeds

SUGGESTED MAP OS Explorer 288 Bradford & Huddersfield

START/FINISH Grid reference: SE222364

DOG FRIENDLINESS Can be off lead on most of walk

PARKING Rodley, by Leeds and Liverpool Canal, close to swing bridge

PUBLIC TOILETS None on route

The Leeds and Liverpool Canal was conceived at a meeting in Bradford in 1766, but it was not until 1770 that the first sod was cut near Liverpool. The ambitious scheme followed a convoluted 127-mile (204km) route across the Pennines, linking many of the important textile towns with the coal pits of Wigan and the western port of Liverpool. From Leeds, via the Aire and Calder Navigation and the River Ouse there was also a continuous waterway to the North Sea ports of Hull and Grimsby. There were several major changes of plan along the way and, in the end, the Leeds and Liverpool required the construction of 91 locks and a 1,640-yard (1,500m) tunnel to broach the summit at Foulridge.

THE GREAT ERA OF THE CANAL

The canal was finally opened end to end in 1816, although intermediate sections were already in use to great effect. The section from Leeds to Skipton opened to a jubilant fanfare on 8 April 1773, and the arrival of two boatloads of coal halved the previous selling price. The ability to transport raw materials and produce quickly and cheaply completely changed the face of this part of England and, with the invention of efficient steam engines, the Industrial Revolution became unstoppable.

The turn of the century saw the country gripped by 'canal mania', and by 1840 almost 4,500 miles (7,242km) of navigable waterway criss-crossed Britain, opening the hinterland to trade and industry. Some canals, like the Leeds and Liverpool, were highly profitable and returned massive fortunes to their backers, but others were purely speculative and realised little, if any return.

DECLINE AND REBIRTH

But the writing was already on the wall. In 1825, the Stockton–Darlington railway opened with the Liverpool–Manchester line following five years later. Unaffected by icy winters or summer drought and able to shift far greater loads at speed, the railway age had arrived. By the end of the 19th century the country had 22,000 miles (35,000km) of railway.

Yet, the canals did not suffer an instant death. Many were taken over and operated by the new railway companies, and trade on the major routes, albeit steadily declining, continued well into the 20th century. However, from the 1950s recreational use reversed the trend, saving some canals from closure while bringing others back from disuse and dereliction. The Leeds and Liverpool remained navigable throughout its length and is today a vibrant corridor linking city hearts to the countryside.

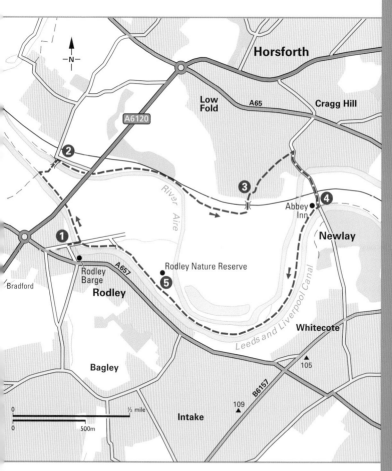

❶ Cross the canal swing bridge, and go left along the broad tow path, passing beneath a bridge carrying the ring road. Reaching a second swing bridge, turn right along a sett-paved

lane. After only 30yds (27m), drop along a stepped path on the left to a lower track. Follow it over a stone bridge spanning the River Aire.

② On the far bank, immediately turn off right down steps to a riverside path. Follow it downstream from the bridge, passing back beneath the main road. Carry on for another 0.5 miles (800m) then, as the river swings away to the right, bear off to a kissing gate. Stick with the higher path, signed to New Laithes Road, which rises at the edge of pasture alongside a deepening railway cutting. Eventually reaching another kissing gate, slip through and continue on a contained path that soon swings across a railway bridge and leads out to a street.

③ Turn right and walk for 0.25 miles (400m). Approaching its eventual end, watch for a stepped path dropping on the right that cuts the corner onto Newlay Lane. Walk down the hill to a bridge crossing the river and continue to a second bridge spanning the railway. Walk on past the Abbey Inn to approach a bridge arching over the canal. Drop left to the tow path.

④ Carry on along the tow path, beneath the bridge to the right. After a mile (1.6km), at the second swing bridge, a track off through gates on the right leads into the Rodley Nature Reserve. Pools, marshland, a willow coppice and hay meadow attract wildfowl and many species of small birds as well as butterflies and dragonflies. The reserve is open on Wednesdays, weekends and most bank holidays and admission is free.

⑤ Walk on beside the canal. It is only just over 0.25 miles (400m) back to the start point.

WHERE TO EAT AND DRINK For refreshments, you have a choice of pubs. The Rodley Barge, at the beginning of the walk, has a small beer garden from which you can enjoy the comings and goings on the canal. Just beyond Newlay Bridge, an early (1819) example of cast iron bridge building, is another characterful hostelry: the Abbey Inn, seemingly marooned between the river and canal.

WHAT TO SEE The canal here, and as far as Armley towards Leeds and Apperley Bridge towards Shipley, has been designated a Site of Special Scientific Interest (SSSI) because of the range of aquatic life it supports. On the surface this includes coots, moorhens, ducks and swans, whilst below the waterline you may spot a pike lurking in the depths. Look out, too, for kingfishers and wagtails.

WHILE YOU'RE THERE Once it has left the centre of Leeds, the Leeds and Liverpool Canal has a surprisingly rural aspect. Smoke-blackened Kirkstall Abbey – founded in 1152 but now a romantic ruin – stands by the River Aire, with the Abbey House Museum on the opposite side of the main A65 road. Both are well worth a visit. The abbey is cared for by Leeds City Council and admission is free. It was home to a community of Cistercian monks who led a self-contained life with little contact from the nearby medieval city of Leeds. After its dissolution in 1539, the roofing, windows and much stonework was appropriated for use in local building works. The museum (charge) has reconstructions of Victorian street scenes, complete with shops, a Sunday school and even an undertaker's workshop. You can walk to the abbey and museum along the tow path.

Standedge from Marsden

DISTANCE 8.25 miles (13.3km)   MINIMUM TIME 4hrs

ASCENT/GRADIENT 1,215ft (370m) ▲▲▲   LEVEL OF DIFFICULTY ✦✦✦

PATHS Old tracks and byways, canal tow path, several stiles

LANDSCAPE Heather moorland

SUGGESTED MAP OS Explorer OL21 South Pennines

START/FINISH Grid reference: SE047118

DOG FRIENDLINESS Keep under control where sheep graze on open moorland

PARKING Standedge Tunnel car park by Marsden Station

PUBLIC TOILETS Peel Street in Marsden town centre

Trans-Pennine travel has, until quite recently, been a hazardous business. Over the centuries many routes have been driven across the hills to link the industrial centres of West Yorkshire and Lancashire. Some paths were consolidated into paved causeways for packhorse traffic and then upgraded to take vehicles. This track, linking the Colne Valley to Rochdale and Milnrow, was known as the Rapes Highway.

THE STANDEDGE TUNNEL

When the Huddersfield Narrow Canal was cut, to provide a link between Huddersfield and Ashton-under-Lyne, there was one major obstacle for the canal builders to overcome – the gritstone bulk of Standedge. There was no way round; the canal had to go through. The Standedge Tunnel, extending from Marsden to Diggle, was a monumental feat of engineering. Costly in every sense, it took 16 years to build and many navvies lost their lives. The result was the longest, highest and deepest canal tunnel in the country.

In an attempt to keep those costs down, the tunnel was cut as narrow as possible, which left no room for a tow path. Towing horses had to be led over the hills to the far end of the tunnel while the bargees had to negotiate Standedge Tunnel using their own muscle power alone. This method, known as 'legging', required them to lie on their backs and push with their feet against the sides and roof of the tunnel and would typically take a back-breaking four hours. Closed to canal traffic for many years, the tunnel was reopened in 2001. It is now a major tourist attraction and includes boat trips and a visitor centre.

A REBELLION IN MARSDEN

In 1812 Marsden became the focus for the 'Luddite' rebellion – a fierce protest against mechanisation in the textile industry. Sixty men were put on trial in York for their part in the troubles; 17 of them were subsequently hanged.

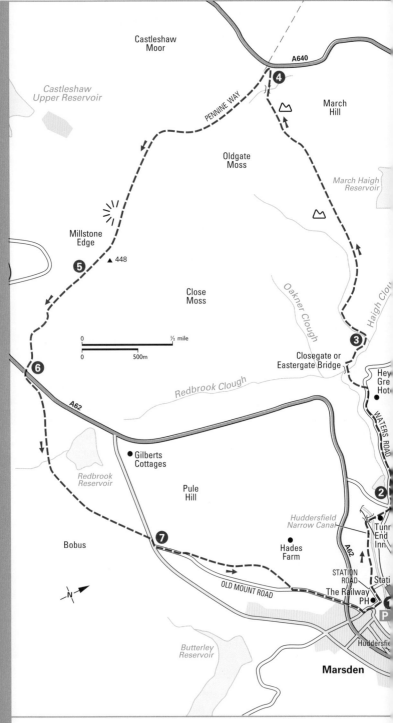

Castleshaw
Moor

A640

Castleshaw
Upper Reservoir

4

March
Hill

PENNINE WAY

Oldgate
Moss

March Haigh
Reservoir

Millstone
Edge

▲ 448

Close
Moss

Oakner Clough

Haigh Clo

3

Closegate or
Eastergate Bridge

5

0   ½ mile
0   500m

6

Hey
Gre
Hot

A62

Redbrook Clough

WATERS ROAD

Gilberts
Cottages

2

Redbrook
Reservoir

Pule
Hill

Huddersfield
Narrow Canal

Tunr
End
Inn

Bobus

7

Hades
Farm

A62

STATION
ROAD

Stati

OLD MOUNT ROAD

The Railway
PH

1

N

P

Butterley
Reservoir

Huddersfie

Marsden

1 From the car park, turn right and then bear right, following the Huddersfield Narrow Canal tow path away from a lock. Approaching Tunnel End, where both canal and railway disappear into tunnels, leave the tow path to cross a footbridge. Bear right uphill past the visitor exhibition to the Tunnel End Inn.

2 Turn left on to Waters Road. Almost immediately, leave through a gate on the left for a path paralleling the road. After rejoining, keep straight ahead past the entrance to the Hey Green Hotel. About 100yds (91m) further on, bear left, just before a cottage, on to a footpath. The path takes you across Closegate Bridge, known locally as Eastergate Bridge, where two becks meet.

3 Swing right, following the beck for about 100yds (91m), before forking left at a waymarker into a narrow side-valley. The path levels higher up, curving towards the rounded prominence of March Hill, now intermittently marked by stone wayposts. After a final stiff pull, the path descends towards the A640.

4 Just before reaching the road, turn sharp left at a Pennine Way sign over a wooden bridge spanning a little beck. The onward path rises and falls over the moss for just over 0.5 miles (800m) to a junction at the abrupt lip of Standedge. Go left along the top of the scarp, enjoying the panoramic view across East Lancashire.

5 Beyond the trig point, the path gently loses height, passing through successive gates and across broken walls to emerge on to a track. Follow it left out to the A62, where a car park overlooks Brun Clough Reservoir.

6 Cross the road and take steps up to the left from the car park. Signed 'Pennine Way', the path parallels the deep road cutting before turning away across Marsden Moor. To the left is Redbrook Reservoir, with Pule Hill beyond. Approaching a marker stone, bear left at a footpath sign, dipping across a stream to continue over the moss. Eventually, after 0.75 miles (1.2km), the way narrows and drops steeply to a stream in a gully. Climb beyond to a road.

7 Turn right and then immediately left on to Old Mount Road. After 50yds (46m), bear left again, along a stony track signed to Hades Farm. After 0.5 miles (800m), watch for a discreetly signed path that descends beside a wall to rejoin Old Mount Road. Continue downhill, crossing the main road into Towngate. Bear left past the church and at the end go left again up Station Road back to the car park.

WHERE TO EAT AND DRINK The cafe by the entrance to the Standedge Tunnel serves light refreshments, or try The Railway by the start of the walk in Marsden, where walkers are very welcome and the food is served daily.

WHAT TO SEE In spring and early summer listen out for a cuckoo. Folklore says that the people of Marsden believed that the cuckoo brought the sunshine. They celebrate Cuckoo Day in April each year.

Overleaf: Brontë Waterfalls on the Brontë Way, Haworth (Walk 32)

Haworth and the Brontë Way

DISTANCE 7.5 miles (12.1km)	**MINIMUM TIME** 3hrs

ASCENT/GRADIENT 968ft (295m) ▲▲▲   **LEVEL OF DIFFICULTY** +++

PATHS Well signed and easy to follow, no stiles

LANDSCAPE Open moorland

SUGGESTED MAP OS Explorer OL21 South Pennines

START/FINISH Grid reference: SE029372

DOG FRIENDLINESS On lead near sheep on open moorland

PARKING Pay-and-display car park, near Brontë Parsonage

PUBLIC TOILETS Central Park, Haworth

Who could have imagined, when the Revd Patrick Brontë became curate of the Church of St Michael and All Angels in 1820, that the little gritstone town of Haworth would become a literary hotspot drawing visitors in great numbers: some to gain an insight into the works of his daughters Charlotte, Emily and Anne, others just to enjoy a day out?

That three prodigious talents were found within one family is remarkable. To have created such great works as *Jane Eyre* and *Wuthering Heights* while living in such a bleakly inhospitable place is almost beyond belief. The public were unprepared for this trio of lady novelists, which is why all the books published during their lifetimes bore the androgynous pen names of Currer, Ellis and Acton Bell.

From the day that Patrick Brontë came to Haworth with his wife and six children, tragedy was never far away. His wife died the following year and two daughters did not live to adulthood. His only son, Branwell, succumbed to drink and drugs; Anne and Emily died aged 29 and 30 respectively. Charlotte, alone, lived long enough to marry. But after just one year of marriage – to her father's curate – she, too, fell ill and died in 1855, at the age of 38. Revd Brontë survived them all, living to the ripe old age of 84. The Georgian parsonage is now a museum, painstakingly restored to reflect the lives of the Brontës and the rooms are filled with their personal treasures.

Tourism is no recent development; by the middle of the 19th century, the first literary pilgrims were finding their way to Haworth. No matter how crowded this little town becomes (and those who value their solitude should avoid visiting on a sunny summer weekend), it is always possible to escape to the moors that surround the town. You can follow, literally, in the footsteps of the three sisters as they sought freedom and inspiration, away from the stifling confines of the parsonage and the adjacent graveyard.

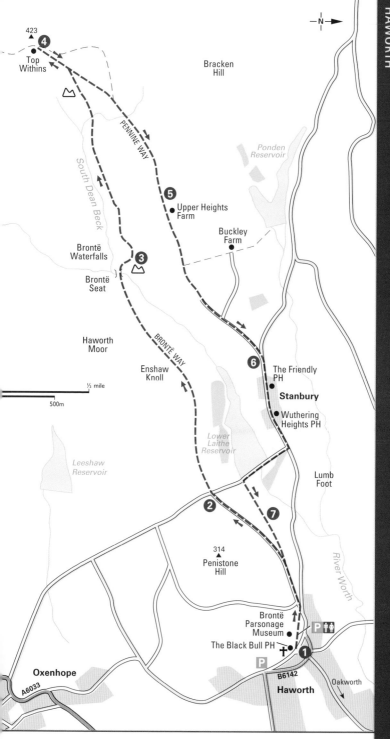

423
▲
4 Top Withins

Bracken Hill

Ponden Reservoir

PENNINE WAY

South Dean Beck

5 Upper Heights Farm

Buckley Farm

Brontë Waterfalls

3 Brontë Seat

BRONTË WAY

Haworth Moor

Enshaw Knoll

½ mile

500m

Lower Laithe Reservoir

6 The Friendly PH

Stanbury

Wuthering Heights PH

Leeshaw Reservoir

Lumb Foot

2

314
▲
Penistone Hill

7

River Worth

Brontë Parsonage Museum

The Black Bull PH

P

1

Oxenhope

A6033

P

B6142

Haworth

Oakworth

1 Take the cobbled lane beside the King's Arms, signed to the Brontë Parsonage Museum. The lane soon becomes a paved field path that leads to the Haworth–Stanbury road. Walk left along the road and, after just 75yds (69m), take a left fork, signed to Penistone Hill. Continue along this quiet road to a T-junction.

2 Follow the track opposite, signed to the Brontë Waterfalls. Becoming a path, it eventually descends to South Dean Beck where, close to the stone bridge, you will find the Brontë Seat (a boulder that resembles a chair) and the Brontë Waterfalls. Cross the bridge and climb steeply uphill to a kissing gate and three-way sign.

3 Keep left, uphill, on a paved path signed 'Top Withins'. Beyond another kissing gate, ignore the later left fork. After dipping across a beck the path leads on, eventually climbing to a signpost by a ruined building. Walk a short distance left, uphill, to visit the ruin of Top Withins, possibly the inspiration for *Wuthering Heights*.

4 Retrace your steps to the signpost, but now keep ahead on a paved path, downhill, signed to Stanbury and Haworth and the Pennine Way. Follow a broad, clear track across the wide expanse of wild Pennine moorland.

5 Carry on for a mile (1.6km) to Upper Heights Farm. At a fork there, bear left with the Pennine Way, shortly passing a second farm. Some 200yds (193m) further on at a junction, the Pennine Way leaves to the left. The route, however, continues with the track ahead signed to Stanbury and Haworth. As other tracks join, the way becomes metalled and leads to the main lane at the edge of Stanbury.

6 Bear right along the road through Stanbury, then take the first road on the right, signed to Oxenhope, and cross the dam of Lower Laithe Reservoir. Immediately beyond the dam, turn left onto a service road and fork right along an uphill track that meets the lane by Haworth Cemetery.

7 From here you retrace your outward route: walk left along the road, soon taking a gap stile on the right, to follow the paved field path back into Haworth.

WHERE TO EAT AND DRINK The Black Bull is Haworth's most famous public house, standing in the little cobbled square at the top of the steep main street. Here, you can have a sandwich, or a snack, or perhaps choose something from the specials board.

WHAT TO SEE The Brontës are extremely popular in Japan, so don't be surprised to find that some signs in the town – and on the walk to Top Withins, too – are written in both English and Japanese. Strange but true.

WHILE YOU'RE THERE At the bottom of that famous cobbled street is Haworth Station, on the restored Keighley and Worth Valley Railway. Take a steam train journey on Britain's last remaining complete branch line railway. Or browse through the books and railway souvenirs at the station shop.

Ilkley Moor and the Twelve Apostles

DISTANCE 4.5 miles (7.2km)	**MINIMUM TIME** 2hrs	

ASCENT/GRADIENT 803ft (245m) ▲▲▲   **LEVEL OF DIFFICULTY** ✚✚✤

PATHS Good moorland paths, some steep paths towards end of walk, no stiles

LANDSCAPE Mostly open heather moorland, and gritstone crags

SUGGESTED MAP OS Explorer 297 Lower Wharfedale

START/FINISH Grid reference: SE132467

DOG FRIENDLINESS Under close control where sheep graze freely on moorland

PARKING Car park below Cow and Calf rocks

PUBLIC TOILETS Beside refreshment kiosk at car park

Ilkley Moor is a long ridge of millstone grit, immediately to the south of Ilkley. With or without a hat, Ilkley Moor is a special place... Not just for walkers, but for lovers of archaeological relics, too. These extensive heather moors are identified on maps as Rombalds Moor, named after a legendary giant. But, thanks to the famous song, Ilkley Moor is how it will always be known.

AN ANCIENT RING

The Twelve Apostles is a ring of Bronze Age standing stones sited close to the meeting of two ancient routes across the moor. If you expect to find something of Stonehenge proportions, you will be disappointed. The twelve slabs of millstone grit (there were more stones originally, probably twenty, with one at the centre) are arranged in a circle approximately 50ft (15m) in diameter. The tallest of the stones is little more than 3ft (1m). The circle is, nevertheless, a genuinely ancient monument.

The Twelve Apostles are merely the most visible evidence of 7,000 years of occupation of these moors. There are other, smaller circles too, and Ilkley Moor is celebrated for its Bronze Age rock carvings, many showing the familiar 'cup and ring' designs. The most famous of these rocks features a sinuous swastika: traditionally a symbol of good luck, until the Nazis corrupted it. There are milestones, dating from more recent times, which would have given comfort and guidance to travellers across these lonely moors. In addition to Pancake and Haystack rocks, seen on this walk, there are dozens of other natural gritstone rock formations. The biggest and best known are the Cow and Calf, close to the start of this walk, where climbers practise their holds and rope work.

A guidebook of 1829 described Ilkley as a little village. It was the discovery of mineral springs that transformed Ilkley into a prosperous

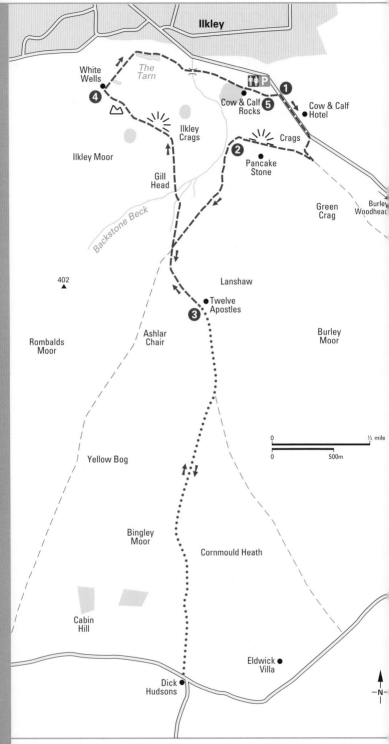

Ilkley

White
Wells

*The
Tarn*

4

Cow & Calf
Rocks

5

1

Cow & Calf
Hotel

Ilkley
Crags

Crags

2

Pancake
Stone

Ilkley Moor

Gill
Head

Green
Crag

Burley
Woodhead

Backstone Beck

402 ▲

Lanshaw

Twelve
Apostles

3

Ashlar
Chair

Burley
Moor

Rombalds
Moor

0 ────────── ½ mile

0 ────────── 500m

Yellow Bog

Bingley
Moor

Cornmould Heath

Cabin
Hill

Eldwick
Villa

Dick
Hudsons

—N—

spa town. Dr William Mcleod arrived here in 1847, recognised the town's potential and spent the next 25 years creating a place where the well-heeled could 'take the waters' in upmarket surroundings. Dr Mcleod recognised the curative properties of cold water and promoted what he called the 'Ilkley Cure', a regime of exercise and cold baths. Luxurious hotels known as 'hydros' sprang up around the town to cater to the influx of visitors.

Predating the town's popularity as a spa is White Wells, built in 1700 around one of the original springs. Some 100 years later plunge baths were added, where people could bathe in cold water. Overlooking the town, White Wells and cafe are open New Year's Day and at weekends in school holidays, whenever the flag is flying.

1 Walk up beside the road, forking right 150yds (138m) beyond the Cow and Calf Hotel onto a signed footpath. Higher up, swing right and then turn left. At a waymark, double back right onto the edge and follow it past the Pancake Stone. Dip across a path rising along a shallow gully and continue beyond Haystack Rock, joining another path from the left. Keep left at successive forks, swinging parallel to the broad fold containing Backstone Beck, over to the right.

2 After gently rising for 0.75 miles (1.2km) across open moor, the path eventually meets the Bradford-Ilkley Dales Way link. Go left along the paved path, cresting the rise by Lanshaw Lad, a prominent boundary stone to reach the Twelve Apostles, lying just beyond.

3 Retrace your steps from the Twelve Apostles, this time staying with the paved Dales Way. Keep ahead beyond the end of the flags, crossing

a small stream and then Backstone Beck at Gill Head. Climbing away, take the left fork past a waymark. After 0.25 miles (400m), keep ahead at a crossing. The path then swings left in a steep descent, eventually leading to White Wells.

4 Swing right in front of the cafe and bath house, the path passing a small pond and slanting down the rocky hillside to meet a metalled path. Go right, taking either branch around the tarn. Leave up steps at the far end, the ongoing path later dipping to cross Backstone Beck. Over the bridge, bear left and stick with the main trail. Approaching the Cow and Calf, ignore a crossing path and keep ahead to skirt below the outcrop.

5 It's worth taking a few minutes to investigate the rocks and watch climbers practising their belays and traverses (climbing techniques). From here a paved path leads back to the car park.

WHILE YOU'RE THERE Ilkley Moor is an intriguingly ancient landscape, criss-crossed by old tracks. This walk and its extension offer short and long options, but you could explore for weeks without walking the same path twice. An east–west walk from the Cow and Calf will take you along the moorland ridge, with terrific views of Ilkley and Wharfedale for most of the way.

Across Ilkley Moor to Dick Hudsons

DISTANCE 8 miles (12.9km)   MINIMUM TIME 3hrs 15min

ASCENT/GRADIENT 1,181ft (360m) ▲▲▲   LEVEL OF DIFFICULTY ✦✦✦

SEE MAP AND INFORMATION PANEL FOR WALK 33

Walk 34 is an extension of Walk 33, continuing beyond the Twelve Apostles stone circle, across Ilkley Moor, to Dick Hudsons. It's a classic walk enjoyed by many generations of ramblers. You can stride out across heather moorland, knowing that no matter what time of the day you arrive (within reason), you should be able to get a meal. Food is served each day from 12 noon to 10pm (9.30pm on Sundays). Dick Hudson, incidentally, was a popular landlord of Queen Victoria's day; the pub's original name was the Fleece Inn.

Continue past the Twelve Apostles to a fork and keep right. Reaching a milestone, take the right branch again, soon passing through a gate in a wall. The way falls across the emptiness of Bingley Moor, part of the much larger expanse of Rombalds Moor, where evocative names reflect use over millennia. Eventually, beyond a second gate, the path leaves the moor, culminating in a walled track to meet the road opposite Dick Hudsons.

A glance at the Ordnance Survey map will reveal a variety of return routes to Ilkley, though they all require some road-walking. The best route is to go back the same way you came, retracing your steps to the Twelve Apostles, then rejoining the route of Walk 33 from Point ❸. Before you leave the crest of the moor you may like to follow the ridge path out to the summit cairn. It leaves left, just past the stone circle as you head back towards Ilkley. On a clear day you'll be rewarded with far-reaching views which take in landmarks including York Minster, Roseberry Topping and the White Horse at Kilburn.

WHERE TO EAT AND DRINK This classic walk across Ilkley Moor almost demands that you follow in the footsteps of generations of walkers, by calling in at Dick Hudsons for a hearty meal. If you've time to wander around Ilkley itself, the first hostelry you'll come to is the Midland Hotel, serving bar meals and real ales. Further along the street, on The Grove, you'll find a branch of the famous Betty's Tea Rooms, where Ilkley ladies mingle with the tourists over tinkling piano music and speciality teas.

Fells of the Holme Valley

DISTANCE 4 miles (6.4km)	MINIMUM TIME 2hrs

ASCENT/GRADIENT 886ft (270m) ▲▲▲   LEVEL OF DIFFICULTY ✦✦✦

PATHS Good tracks most of the way, several stiles

LANDSCAPE Rolling countryside

SUGGESTED MAP OS Explorer 288 Bradford & Huddersfield

START/FINISH Grid reference: SE163067

DOG FRIENDLINESS Keep on lead near livestock and roads

PARKING Lay-by at foot of Town Gate in Hepworth

PUBLIC TOILETS None on route

Presiding over two of the tributary folds that come together in the Holme Valley, Hepworth is one of many villages in this corner of the West Yorkshire Pennines that have retained both charm and communal identity.

AN ANCIENT HERITAGE

The name is of Saxon origin, perhaps identified with a local chief Heppa or merely meaning a settlement occupying the high ground. Handloom weaving and farming were the traditional occupations and determined the style of the houses. Weavers' cottages were usually two or three stories high, with the loom room occupying the whole length of the attic. Rows of narrow, mullioned windows flooded light into the room, which was often reached by an outside staircase and a 'taking in' door. This not only facilitated bringing yarn in and taking the finished cloth pieces out, but also enabled segregation of work from family.

That the weavers were also farmers and small holders remains evident in the village layout, with long, narrow fields falling behind the old cottages. While staple crops could be grown, the land and climate were generally unsuited to agriculture and farming centred upon dairy cattle and the production of sheep, primarily for wool. But the local wool was coarse and, in time, fine wool was imported to produce quality cloths.

Beyond the village, farms were based upon laithe-houses, buildings that combined accommodation, a hay and cattle barn and an upper weaving room under one roof. Examples of these characterful buildings still dot the hillsides around the valley.

THE GREAT PLAGUE

Hepworth was the most northerly place touched by London's Great Plague in 1666. As at Eyam, 20 miles (32km) to the south, the infection arrived in a bolt of cloth. In an effort to stem the contagion, the community threw up a barricade to isolate the afflicted within one half of the village. When normality returned, the thirteen dead were remembered in the planting of trees, one for each departed soul. They still stand (albeit with two replacements) by the village football pitch. The passing of the plague is celebrated today in the Hepworth Feast on the last Monday in June, when villagers process to neighbouring Scholes.

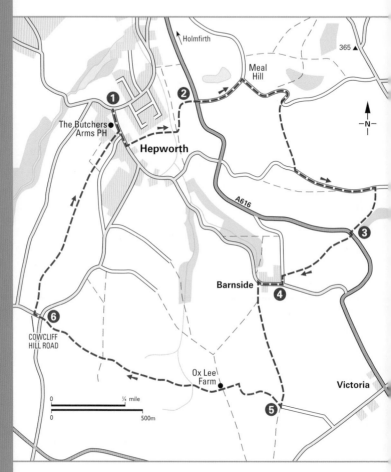

① Walk south along Town Gate past The Butchers Arms. Some 100yds (91m) beyond, look for steps dropping left beside the end of a terrace from which a path falls steeply along the edge of a narrow field. Towards the bottom, slip over a stile and continue to a bridge spanning the stream at the base of the valley. Walk forward to a crossing path and go left to a fork. Branch right up a stepped path, eventually emerging onto the main road.

② Cross to Meal Hill Lane opposite, following it beyond houses to a T-junction. Turn right up the hill past the entrance of Bank House Farm. The way climbs on as a rough track, shortly swinging right. Where it subsequently bends sharp left, leave over a stile on the right. A trod takes the route more easily across the hillside, in time passing through a gate and stile. Keep ahead as a track joins from the right, walking for another 0.25 miles (400m). Approaching a farmstead, half hidden behind trees, watch for a stile on the right. Drop half right across the steep slope to a gate and continue down by the right boundary. Swinging right towards the bottom, it leads out over a final stile onto the road.

❸ Go left 30yds (27m) to a small gate on the right beside a house drive. Cross a paddock to another gate in the far corner and accompany the fence downhill. Through a squeeze gap beyond the base of the dip, follow the ongoing boundary across the fields to cottages above Barnside. Over a final stile, go left past them out to a lane.

❹ Turn right through the hamlet. Just beyond cottages at the bottom look for a stile set back from the lane on the left. Walk away, climbing past the indented corner of a wall.

Continue beside it to a gate at the top. Cross the next field to a stile and climb the rough hillside beyond to another stile beside a gate in the top boundary. Keep the same line past a redundant stile to meet a crossing track along the top of the hill.

❺ Follow it right, through a gate beneath power cables and down to a second gate. The onward path curves right and left above a gully, dropping to a junction of tracks by the abandoned ruin of Ox Lee Farm. Go forward along a walled track. Although occasionally wet and overgrown in places, a parallel path on the right avoids the worst spots. Carry on as the going improves, eventually emerging at a junction of lanes.

❻ Cross to Cowcliff Hill Road opposite. After 50yds (46m) leave over a stile on the right. Follow the wall away to another stile and then continue across successive fields back towards Hepworth, ultimately coming out between buildings by The Butchers Arms.

WHERE TO EAT AND DRINK The Butchers Arms, a real locals' pub in the middle of Hepworth village, is the place for a drink and good food. The White Horse Inn at Jackson Bridge – just north of Hepworth, off the A616 – may be familiar even to first-time visitors, since it has featured in many episodes of *Last of the Summer Wine*. Pictures taken from the comedy series are displayed inside.

WHAT TO SEE The little stone village of Hepworth is surrounded by some of the finest countryside in the county; quiet lanes, stone walls and a wide choice of old paths to walk. The proximity of town and country is a striking feature of the area. You can be walking on tarmac and cobbles, but within a few minutes you can be out on the tops.

WHILE YOU'RE THERE Nearby Jackson Bridge is a cramped little community, wedged into a valley around the White Horse Inn. Here you will find rows of distinctive weavers' cottages. To save space, some houses are built on top of each other, providing 'underdwellings' and 'overdwellings', a building solution more familiar in places like Hebden Bridge.

Oxenhope and the Worth Valley Railway

DISTANCE 6.5 miles (10.4km) MINIMUM TIME 2hrs 45min

ASCENT/GRADIENT 1,148ft (350m) ▲▲▲ LEVEL OF DIFFICULTY ✦✦✦

PATHS Good paths and tracks

LANDSCAPE Upland scenery, moor and pasture

SUGGESTED MAP OS Explorer OL21 South Pennines

START/FINISH Grid reference: SE032353

DOG FRIENDLINESS Keep on lead along country lanes and near livestock

PARKING Street parking in Oxenhope, near Keighley and Worth Valley Railway station

PUBLIC TOILETS None on route

Oxenhope is the terminus of the Keighley and Worth Valley Railway and also the last village in the Worth Valley. To the north are Haworth and Keighley; going south, into Calderdale and Hebden Bridge, requires you to gear down for a scenic drive over the lonely heights of Cock Hill.

Oxenhope was a farming community that expanded with the textile industry. The mills have mostly disappeared and, apart from the railway, the village is best known for the Oxenhope Straw Race, held each year on the first Sunday in July. Competitors have to carry a bale of straw all around the village, while drinking as much beer as possible. Whoever finishes this assault course first is the winner, but it is the local charities that benefit most.

KEIGHLEY AND WORTH VALLEY RAILWAY

The Keighley and Worth Valley line, running for 5 miles (8km) from Keighley to Oxenhope, is one of the longest established private railways in the country, and the last remaining complete branch line. It was built in 1867, funded by local mill owners, but the trains were run by the Midland Railway to link to the main Leeds–Skipton line at Keighley.

When the line fell victim to Dr Beeching's axe in 1962, local rail enthusiasts banded together in opposition. The preservation society bought the line and a major restoration of the line and the stations began. By 1968 the society began running a regular timetable of trains that has continued ever since. Steam trains run every weekend throughout the year, and daily in summer. But the line doesn't just cater to tourists; locals in the Worth Valley appreciate the diesel services into Keighley which operate on almost 200 days per year.

The line runs through the heart of Brontë country, with stations at Oxenhope, Haworth, Oakworth, Danems, Ingrow and Keighley. The stations are a particular delight: fully restored, gas-lit and redolent of the age of steam. So when Edith Nesbitt's classic children's novel, *The Railway Children*, was being filmed in 1970, the Keighley and Worth Valley Railway was a natural location choice. Oakworth station – a fine example of an Edwardian station – is the one used in the film. Everyone who has seen the film (it seems to be etched deeply into the national psyche) will enjoy revisiting this much-loved place.

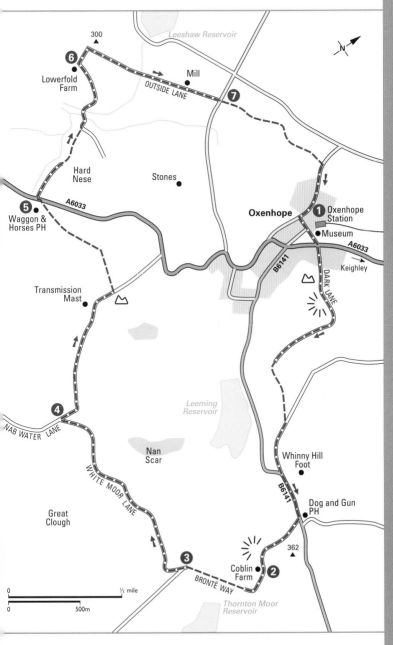

1 Begin along the minor lane beside the entrance of Oxenhope Station, which rises past the overflow car park to the A6033. Cross to Dark Lane opposite and climb steeply away. Later degrading to a track, it eventually ends at a lane. Go right down to the Denholme road (B6141) and follow it left to the Dog and Gun. Turn right opposite the pub into Sawood Lane.

2 At Coblin Farm, your route becomes a rough track. Through a gate at the end, join a metalled track and go right, signed Brontë Way. Keep ahead past the entrance to Thornton Moor Reservoir, passing through a field gate along an unmade track. Ignore the Brontë Way, which then shortly drops off to the right.

3 At a fork 50yds (46m) further on, bear right before a gate on a descending track by the wall. It meanders for a mile (1.6km), passing a clump of trees and then crossing a watercourse before eventually meeting a moorland lane.

4 Go right here, eventually passing a cattle grid and a telecommunications mast. Carry on for another 150yds (137m) but, as the road begins a steep descent, take a wall stile on the left. Later, through another wall stile, walk left, uphill, on a broad, walled track that deposits you at the Waggon and Horses Inn.

5 Walk left, leaving after 30yds (27m) by a signpost on the right to a steeply descending track. Levelling after 300yds (274m), it swings right. Cross a stile by a gate on the left. Slant right down a couple of fields and continue the line across rough ground, dropping to a walled path at the bottom. Go left across a stream and climb away to Lowerfold Farm.

6 Walk forward past a row of cottages and go right on a metalled track. Follow it away down the hill above the Leeshaw Reservoir for 0.75 miles (1.2km). After passing a converted mill, it finally leads out to a lane.

7 Cross the lane and take the track ahead (signed to Marsh). Pass right of the end house, on a narrow walled path and continue across a small field. Through a courtyard, go left and right past cottages. Emerging, take the kissing gate opposite, from which a path runs through to a walled track. To the right it leads past houses, across a field and out past more houses to a road. Go right back down into Oxenhope.

WHERE TO EAT AND DRINK The Waggon and Horses Inn is at the walk's halfway point, on the Hebden Bridge Road out of Oxenhope. It enjoys great views over the valley and has a reputation for its good food. If you take the train, there's an excellent cafe at Oxenhope Station in a stationary British Rail buffet car. It's open weekends and during the school holidays.

WHILE YOU'RE THERE Take a trip to Haworth and back on the Keighley and Worth Valley Railway. You can return on foot along the Worth Way.

Laycock and Goose Eye

DISTANCE 8 miles (12.9km)	**MINIMUM TIME** 3hrs 15min

ASCENT/GRADIENT 1,230ft (375m) ▲▲△   **LEVEL OF DIFFICULTY** +++

PATHS Good paths and tracks, take care with route finding

LANDSCAPE Wooded valley and heather moorland

SUGGESTED MAP OS Explorer OL21 South Pennines

START/FINISH Grid reference: SE032410

DOG FRIENDLINESS Under close control where sheep graze on sections of moorland

PARKING In Laycock village, roadside parking at Keighley end of village, close to the village hall

PUBLIC TOILETS None on route

To the west of Keighley a tranche of moorland sits astride the border between Yorkshire and Lancashire. Here you can walk for miles without seeing another hiker – and perhaps with just curlew and grouse for company. When we think of textile mills, we tend to associate them with cramped towns full of smoking chimneys. But the earliest mills were sited in surprisingly rural locations, often in the little steep-sided valleys known as cloughs where fast-flowing becks and rivers could be dammed and diverted to turn the waterwheels. There are reminders, in wooded Newsholme Dean, that even a watercourse as small as Dean Beck could be harnessed to provide power to a cotton mill in Goose Eye. Weirs along the beck helped to maintain a good head of water, and one of the mill dams is now popular with anglers.

LAYCOCK AND GOOSE EYE

The village of Laycock contains a number of handsome old houses in the typical South Pennine style including an attractive ribbon of terraced houses that were built into the steep hillside in the early 19th century. While Laycock sits in an elevated position on the hillside, with good valley views, neighbouring Goose Eye nestles deep in a hollow. The village was originally called Goose Heights, which the local dialect contracted to 'Goose Ay', and thence to the name we know today. Lovers of real ale will already be familiar with the name, as this is the home of the Goose Eye Brewery.

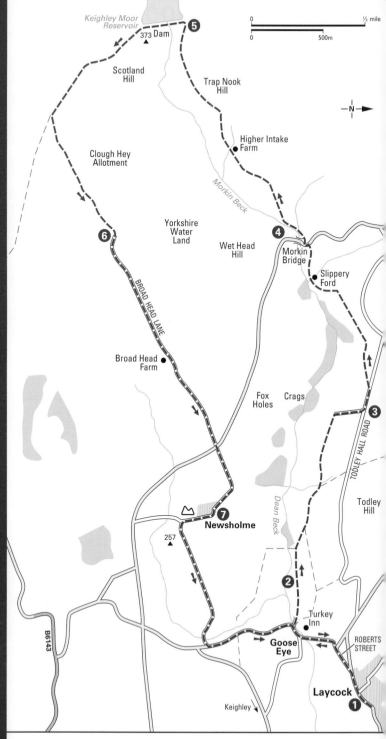

Keighley Moor
Reservoir

5

373 Dam

Scotland
Hill

Trap Nook
Hill

Higher Intake
Farm

Clough Hey
Allotment

Morkin Beck

Yorkshire
Water
Land

Wet Head
Hill

4

Morkin
Bridge

Slippery
Ford

6

BROAD HEAD LANE

Broad Head
Farm

Fox
Holes

Crags

TODLEY HALL ROAD

3

Todley
Hill

Dean Beck

7

Newsholme

257

2

Turkey
Inn

B6143

Goose
Eye

ROBERTS
STREET

1

Laycock

Keighley

½ mile

500m

N

1 Walk through the village of Laycock. Where the road narrows, go left down a paved track, Roberts Street. Beyond terraced houses, descend along a narrow walled path to emerge on to a road, which you follow down into Goose Eye. Pass the Turkey Inn. Just 50yds (46m) after you cross Dean Beck, take the steps on your right and re-cross the beck on a footbridge. Follow the beck upstream and take a footbridge on the right, across the now-dry mill leat.

2 Carry on up the wooded valley, later passing through a gap in a wall. Ignore a path off right and keep ahead, breaking onto open hillside. Before long, the way passes behind a farmhouse to join a farm track. Go left but then branch right on a rough track signed to Slippery Ford. Carry on through a gate, later fording a stream. Just beyond, fork right on a rising hollow path, which later becomes a track. Eventually swinging right it climbs to meet a road.

3 Walk left along the road for 75yds (68m) before taking an access track on the left leading down to Bottoms Farm. Entering the yard, waymarks indicate a small gate to the right. Skirt beside a barn to a stile from which a path to the left continues across the hillside. Through a gate, carry on over stiles across a succession of fields. At the far side of the fourth field, drop left to find a confluence of two streams. Ford the side beck to a gate and carry on at the edge of another field above the main stream. Reaching the field corner, turn up beside the wall, climbing to a gate near the top of the rise beside Slitheroford Farm.

Walk through the yard and out to a lane. Follow the road down to the left to the beck at Morkin Bridge.

4 Reaching Morkin Bridge, turn off right to follow a metalled track through a gate. It rises steadily onto the moors above the fold of Morkin Beck, passing Higher Intake Farm and eventually leading out to Keighley Moor Reservoir.

5 Walk left, across the top of the dam. At the far end, ignore the signed track to the right and instead bear left at a concrete post along a gently descending moorland track. At a boggy section keep ahead, the vague path eventually becoming more distinct as it joins a wall. Follow it for 150yds (137m) to a gateway, turn though and then bear half right to cross line of grouse butts on a distinct but narrow path through the heather. Eventually, on meeting a track, follow it right over a cattle grid.

6 Soon leaving the moorland behind, Broad Head Lane runs straight for 0.75 miles (1.2km). Meeting a road by a farm, cross to a track opposite and follow it to cottages at Newsholme.

7 Wind forward between the houses and follow a lane downhill. After 250yds (229m), opposite the entrance to Green End Farm, turn left. Degrading to a track, the way eventually swings across a beck to meet a road. Follow it left down to Goose Eye and the Turkey Inn. Carry on steeply uphill to where the lane swings sharp left, there branching off right to reverse your outward route up Robert Street back to Laycock.

WHERE TO EAT AND DRINK The Turkey Inn in Goose Eye is a splendid village pub and has a very good reputation for food.

Along the Colne Valley

DISTANCE 7 miles (11.3km)   MINIMUM TIME 3hrs 30min

ASCENT/GRADIENT 900ft (275m) ▲▲▲   LEVEL OF DIFFICULTY ✦✦✦

PATHS Field paths, good tracks and canal tow path, many stiles

LANDSCAPE Typical South Pennine rough pasture, canalside

SUGGESTED MAP OS Explorer OL21 South Pennines

START/FINISH Grid reference: SE079140

DOG FRIENDLINESS Tow path is especially good for dogs

PARKING Plenty of street parking in Slaithwaite

PUBLIC TOILETS Slaithwaite and Marsden

Transport across the Pennine watershed has always presented problems. The Leeds and Liverpool Canal, built during the 1770s, took a convoluted route across the Pennines, through the Aire Gap at Skipton. Then came the Rochdale Canal, a more direct route, but this canal has more locks than any other inland waterway in the country. However, with the increase in trade between Yorkshire and Lancashire, a third route across the Pennines was soon needed. The Huddersfield Narrow Canal links Huddersfield with Ashton-under-Lyne in Greater Manchester. Begun in 1798, the canal was opened to traffic in 1811. Though only 20 miles (32.2km) long, it includes the Standedge Tunnel.

BEADS ON A STRING

The Colne Valley, to the west of Huddersfield, is representative of industrial West Yorkshire. Towns with evocative names – Milnsbridge, Linthwaite, Slaithwaite and Marsden – are threaded along the River Colne. In the 18th century this was a landscape of scattered farms and handloom weavers, mostly situated on the higher ground. As with Calderdale, a few miles to the north, the deep-cut valley of the Colne was transformed by the Industrial Revolution. Once the textile processes began to be mechanised, mills were built in the valley bottom by industrial entrepreneurs. They specialised in the production of fine worsted cloth.

The River Colne provided the power for the first mills, and the canal subsequently improved the transport links. The mills grew larger as water power gave way to steam, towering over the rows of terraced houses built in their shadows. Throughout this walk you can see the mill chimneys and the sawtooth roof-lines of the weaving sheds, though some mills are ruinous and others are now given over to other trades.

Slaithwaite (often pronounced 'Slowitt') is typical of the textile towns in the Colne Valley: unpretentious, a little bit scruffy. Now, with the canal restored, Slaithwaite has a new lease of life.

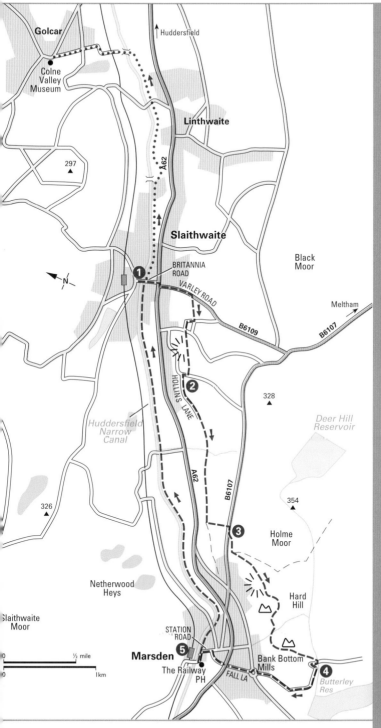

Golcar

↑ Huddersfield

Colne
Valley
Museum

Linthwaite

A62

297 ▲

Slaithwaite

Black
Moor

N

BRITANNIA
ROAD

❶

VARLEY ROAD

Meltham

B6109

B6107

HOLLINS LANE

❷

328 ▲

Deer Hill
Reservoir

Huddersfield
Narrow
Canal

A62

B6107

326 ▲

354 ▲

❸

Holme
Moor

Netherwood
Heys

Hard
Hill

Slaithwaite
Moor

½ mile

1 km

STATION
ROAD

❺

Marsden

The Railway
PH

FALL LA

Bank Bottom
Mills

❹

Butterley
Res

1 Begin along Britannia Road, turning right on to the A62 and crossing to continue up Varley Road. Beyond the last house, go through a squeeze gap on the right and climb to a field. Swinging right and left, follow an indistinct path to a stile on the opposite side. Carry on beside the right-hand wall, crossing a stile to a lane. Follow it right and left to a crossroads. Take the track opposite, bearing left after 20yds (18m) on to another track between houses. Go over a stile at the end and keep ahead at the edge of successive fields, crossing more stiles and eventually leaving beside a house on to a lane.

2 Go briefly right before turning left along a track that ultimately leads to a farm. Walk forwards past the front of a cottage, passing through a dilapidated gate into a field corner. Carry on ahead, negotiating gates either side of a beck at the far side. Climb a stile and pass an abandoned farmstead to a walled path. Where the path shortly veers right, take the gate ahead into a field. Follow the right wall, bearing slightly left beyond its end to slant up across rough pastures. Go over a stile and keep forwards, soon crossing a second stile on to a walled path. Climb left to another stile, then turn right down to a bend. Scaling a wall stile on the left, walk away at the bottom edge of fields to a kissing gate. Continue through a plantation, swinging left at the far side along a path up to the B6107.

3 Walk right for 75yds (69m), then take a track off to the left. Continue past a house and through a gate, shortly reaching a fork. Keep ahead on the right branch. Cross a beck and fork left uphill; the way narrows to a path. At a junction turn right to pass below old quarries on the shoulder of Hard Hill. Climb to a kissing gate, then drop to a bridge beside a stone aqueduct. After rising to a memorial bench, the way levels and Butterley Reservoir comes into view. Beyond another kissing gate by a small stone building, climb left to a stile, carrying on over a second stile and out on to a metalled track. Follow it down to a lane.

4 Continue downhill, eventually passing terraced houses dwarfed by Bank Bottom Mills. Keep straight ahead at a roundabout along Fall Lane, bearing left before the end to pass beneath the main road. Keep left over a bridge and then right past the church. At the end walk left up Station Road.

5 Join the Huddersfield Narrow Canal tow path opposite The Railway pub. Follow it right, dropping past the first of many locks, for a pleasant 3-mile (4.8km) walk along the tow path back to Slaithwaite.

WHERE TO EAT AND DRINK The Railway, close to the rail station and canal in Marsden, comes at the halfway point of the walk, while the Moonraker Floating Tea Room is housed on a narrowboat moored at the end.

Up the Ginnels to Golcar

DISTANCE 4 miles (6.4km)   MINIMUM TIME 2hrs 30min

ASCENT/GRADIENT 377ft (115m) ▲▲▲   LEVEL OF DIFFICULTY ✚✚✚

SEE MAP AND INFORMATION PANEL FOR WALK 38

An extension to Walk 38 can be made by continuing through Slaithwaite. Follow the tow path's southern bank, soon leaving the town. After 1.5 miles (2.4km), at bridge 38, cross the canal and climb through a wood and underneath a railway viaduct. The ongoing track winds around a small estate, but at the second right bend, keep ahead up a narrow ginnel past a cemetery and Baptist church. Meeting a road, carry on along the street opposite, following it all the way up the hill to emerge on a main road in front of the parish church. Golcar's fascinating museum is to the left down a narrow street.

Though only 3 miles (4.8km) from the centre of Huddersfield, the hilltop village of Golcar has managed to keep its identity. The village boasts a number of well-preserved hand-weavers' cottages, which provided living and working accommodation under one roof.

The top storeys were typically south-facing, with long rows of mullioned windows, which allowed as much light as possible into the loom chambers. Four of these cottages have been amalgamated to form the Colne Valley Museum, open weekend and bank holiday afternoons. Here you can get a good impression of what life was like for weavers and their families, before the textile industries developed on a truly industrial scale, and production shifted from hilltop villages to the mill towns in the valley. There's a loom chamber, weaver's living room, gaslit clogger's shop and much more. After investigating the ginnels, weavers' cottages and the Colne Valley Museum, retrace your steps down to the canal, and follow it back to Slaithwaite.

WHERE TO EAT AND DRINK There is a wide choice of pubs and cafes in both Slaithwaite and Marsden. The Railway, close to the rail station and canal, in Marsden, comes at the halfway point of Walk 38, while Golcar's museum serves drinks.

WHAT TO SEE When Enoch and James Taylor of Marsden started manufacturing cropping frames, they caused consternation amongst the shearers, who feared for their livelihoods. They realised that a single machine could do the work of many men. So, banded together as 'Luddites', the shearers attacked the mills where the hated frames were being introduced. The grave of Enoch Taylor can be seen on Walk 38, on a small green you pass shortly after walking under the A62 and into Marsden.

A stroll through Judy Woods

DISTANCE 3.5 miles (5.7km)	MINIMUM TIME 1hr 15min

ASCENT/GRADIENT 394ft (120m) ▲▲▲   LEVEL OF DIFFICULTY ✚✚✚

PATHS Good tracks and woodland paths

LANDSCAPE Arable land and beech woods

SUGGESTED MAP OS Explorer 288 Bradford & Huddersfield

START/FINISH Grid reference: SE147268

DOG FRIENDLINESS Can be off lead in woods

PARKING On Station Road (off the A641 at Wyke) near information panel and kissing gate leading into Judy Woods

PUBLIC TOILETS None on route

Set within the deep fold of Royd Hall Beck, Judy Woods is a fragment of a once extensive forest that stretched to the Midlands. It survives as one of the finest semi-natural woodlands in the county and is a haven for all manner of wildlife.

AN INDUSTRIAL PAST

The valley's steep sides saved it from historical clearance for agriculture, but the underlying geology attracted a different sort of activity – mining for coal and later iron ore. Initially, from the medieval period, it was undertaken on a small scale in the form of shallow bell pits, whose remains can still be found amongst the trees in the crater-like hollows of collapsed workings. But mechanisation towards the end of the 18th century enabled deeper mines and the area was taken over to supply raw material for the Low Moor Iron Company, which manufactured a whole range of products including some of the cannon used at the Battle of Waterloo. Over 25 miles of wagonway were laid through the woods to transport coal and ore to the nearby factory and many of the embankments and inclines are still visible today.

BEECH PLANTINGS

One of the delightful features of the woodland is the preponderance of massive beech trees, which produce a magnificent spectacle of colour each autumn. Planted during the 18th century, these too were intended for profit – to provide wood for the manufacture of bobbins and spindles for the local textile industry. Despite their majestic appearance, their dense foliage shades the ground to the detriment of other species and they are gradually being replaced by the native birch and oak that would have formed the original woodland cover.

A VICTORIAN PLEASURE GARDEN

Some time after the beech were planted, the area was opened as a pleasure garden. It acquired the name Judy Woods after Judy North, who lived in a cottage by Horse Close Bridge, a packhorse bridge across the stream now known as Judy Bridge. Her husband had been employed as gardener on the estate and, after his death, Judy and her son continued in his stead. To augment their income, Judy began selling refreshments to the visitors and was variously called Stick o'Judy, from the sweets she sold, or 'Gurt' Judy because of her ample proportions.

The woods are now managed for the benefit of wildlife and attract a rich variety of birds. In summer, migrant warblers such as blackcap, chiffchaff and willow warbler arrive from Africa, while in winter, fieldfare and redwing come from the north. Owls, woodpeckers, nuthatches and many garden birds can be spotted all year round. Look out too for roe deer and bats. Spring is particularly beautiful for the bluebells that carpet the glades. Autumn is the time, not only for the turning leaves, but also fungi, which can be found in profusion through the valley.

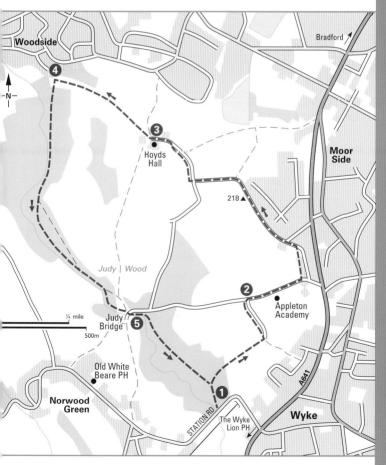

1 From the upper entrance to the woods on Station Road, where there is a notice board and kissing gate, follow a path into the trees signed to Woodside. Where it subsequently swings left, turn off right, walking to a stile at the edge of the trees. Head away across open ground, following an old incline that rises towards a high fence surrounding the perimeter of Appleton Academy. Go left, passing through a gate and continuing out to a lane.

2 Turn right up the hill, walking as far as the entrance to the school. There, turn left onto an unadopted street, Carr House Gate. Follow it past houses to its very end by a breaker's yard. Keep ahead to pick up a path that passes behind more houses. Swinging beneath the foot of communication masts it continues between open fields. Meeting a track, go right to Royds Hall.

3 Follow the track between cottages and an old stable block. Immediately after it swings right past the entrance to the farm, leave over a wall stile on the left. Walk away on a shallow angle to find another stile set left of the far corner. Carry on beside a wall on the right, continuing forward beyond its end within a fringe of beech trees. Keep ahead until you reach a kissing gate leading out to houses.

4 However, instead of passing through, swing left on a path towards Judy Woods. Go through the kissing gate there and follow a good path into the trees. Eventually the gravel way peters out, but keep ahead, now gently descending on a rougher path. Later becoming stepped, it drops to a plank bridge across a stream. Cross and follow Royd Hall Beck to Judy Bridge, a short distance downstream.

5 Climb to the track above and follow it left uphill. However, a short distance along slip through a gap in the right wall to continue on a parallel path. At the top, swing right and walk away, again on a gravel path that wends along the broad crest of the wood. Eventually reaching the junction passed at the start of the walk, go right back to Station Road.

WHERE TO EAT AND DRINK At the junction of the A58 with the A641 near the start of the walk, you'll find The Wyke Lion, which serves real ales and meals in traditional surroundings. Closer to Norwood Green is the Old White Beare. Originally a farmhouse in 1533, it was rebuilt after a fire 60 years later with timbers from an Elizabethan galleon called the White Beare.

WHAT TO SEE In the spring these beech woods are carpeted with bluebells. From late April until early June, the succulent green stems rise up to as much as 18in (45cm) in height. The individual flowers are similar to those of the garden hyacinth.

WHILE YOU'RE THERE This walk brings you close to the centre of Bradford, granted city status in 1897 to acknowledge its importance as 'wool capital of the world'. The city centre has some fine architecture as well as many interesting museums and art galleries.

Exploring Rishworth Moor

DISTANCE 7.5 miles (12.1km)   **MINIMUM TIME** 3hrs

ASCENT/GRADIENT 1,115ft (340m) ▲▲▲   **LEVEL OF DIFFICULTY** +++

PATHS Moorland paths; may be boggy after rain, no stiles

LANDSCAPE Open moorland

SUGGESTED MAP OS Explorer OL21 South Pennines

START/FINISH Grid reference: SE011190

DOG FRIENDLINESS Keep on lead near livestock

PARKING Car beside A58 at Baitings Reservoir

PUBLIC TOILETS None on route

Beginning in the upper reaches of the Ryburn Valley, the walk sets out across the dam of Baitings Reservoir, built in 1956 to supply Wakefield. Climbing Rishworth Moor onto Blackwood Edge, the view opens across the neighbouring valley to the M62 Motorway as it rises from Scammonden across the flank of Moss Moor to cross the Pennine watershed beneath Windy Hill just south of Blackstone Edge. One of the unusual features of the M62 is the division of east- and west-bound carriageways around Stott Hall Farm: the hillside geology is just too unstable to support adjacent carriageways.

AN ANCIENT AND MODERN ROUTE

The South Pennine hills, straddling the Yorkshire/Lancashire boundary and watershed, have long been a great obstacle to travel. A fascinating paved road climbs steeply up Blackstone Edge; opinions are divided as to whether it is Roman or a medieval packhorse track. But no one was in any doubt that this was difficult terrain. The redoubtable traveller, Celia Fiennes, coming this way in 1698, described this route as '...a dismal high precipice, steep in ascent'. Daniel Defoe came the same way in August 1724, during a blizzard that was unseasonal even for the Pennines.

A succession of turnpike roads were built in the 18th and early 19th centuries. Yet it was as recently as the 1970s, with the building of the M62 motorway, that trans-Pennine travel became routine. Surveyors did some of their initial work using ponies: the easiest mode of transport in this inhospitable landscape. As drivers now cruise effortlessly across the empty moors, it's easy to forget what a feat of engineering it was to build 'the motorway in the clouds'. At an altitude of 1,220ft (372m), the M62 is the highest motorway in the country, and this Pennine section offers some dramatic features.

When built, Scammonden Bridge was the largest single-span bridge in Europe and carries the B6114 across the motorway. Less obvious to motorway users is the Scammonden Dam just to the east. It is the only reservoir embankment in Britain to carry a motorway and the lake it created flooded a dozen farms in the Deanhead Valley. Having taken five years to build, the motorway was opened to traffic in 1970. It may be easier to traverse the Pennines today, but the weather here is notoriously unpredictable, and few years pass without the traffic seizing up in winter's icy grip.

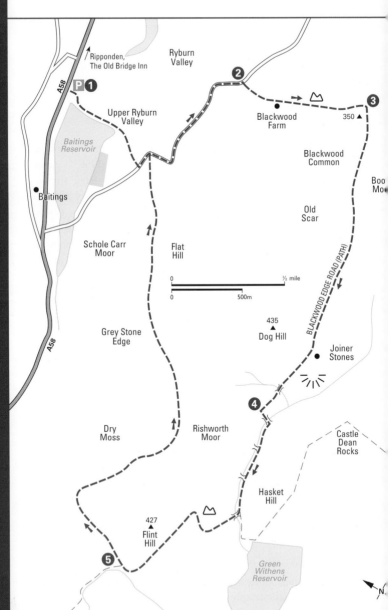

1 Take the path across the dam, a track beyond climbing past a farm to a lane. Turn left and walk for 0.5 miles (800m) to go over a bridge. Some 50yds (46m) after swinging over the bridge, change tack and through a waymarked gate in the right-hand wall.

2 Follow a tumbledown wall uphill towards Blackwood Farm. Entering between outbuildings, walk beyond the farmhouse to a gate at the top of the yard. Walk up the next field to a gate and continue steeply uphill, following the wall on your left. Look for views of the Ryburn Valley as you approach the crest of the hill. You will come to a ladder stile, next to a gate in the wall.

3 Don't cross, but strike off right over rough moorland; the path is distinct but narrow. Occasional yellow-topped markers confirm the route, which runs roughly parallel to the M62, aiming to the right of a tall mast on the far side of the motorway. After a mile (1.6km), the path begins a gentle descent, giving good views down to Green Withens Reservoir ahead. Keep going forward above the head of a gully then over a plank bridge as the path falls across the hill to a bridge spanning a reservoir catchment channel.

4 Cross and walk right, following this watercourse towards the reservoir. Ignore the next two bridges across, but at the third, which is about 300yds (274m) before the reservoir embankment and waymarked 'Blackstone Edge and Baitings', revert to the northern bank. Bear slightly left to follow a path uphill – soon quite steeply – before it levels and swings left around Flint Hill. It later curves right to crest the watershed into the Upper Ryburn Valley where there is a junction of paths by a water channel.

5 Go right here (a sign indicates Baitings Reservoir), continuing to skirt the hill on a good, level path. After a mile (1.6km), watch for a fork marked by a wooden post and bear left, gradually descending towards Baitings Reservoir. When you come to a wall corner, keep straight ahead, following the wall on your left. A developing track leads out to the lane. Go left and take the second right, reversing your outward steps to the car park.

WHERE TO EAT AND DRINK Take the opportunity to visit one of the oldest (it dates to the 14th century) and most delightful pubs in West Yorkshire. The Old Bridge Inn is tucked out of sight off the main A58 road, on a cobbled lane near the church, just beyond an old packhorse bridge. Real ale, picturesque surroundings and excellent food make the pub rather special.

WHAT TO SEE The upland moors of the South Pennines are important Sites of Special Scientific Interest (SSSI), with sparse landscapes of heather, grasses, bilberry, cotton grass and crowberry, where birds such as merlin and golden plover still thrive. The only thing lacking here, apart from trees, is people – you can stride out across these moors for mile after mile without seeing another walker.

WHILE YOU'RE THERE The Ryburn Valley branches off from the Calder at Sowerby Bridge. Ripponden is a little straggle of a town that's well worth exploring. It was once an important weaving centre, known for its dark 'Navy Blue' cloth; at one time it was the sole supplier to the Royal Navy.

Along Langfield Edge to Stoodley Pike

DISTANCE 8.5 miles (13.7km)	**MINIMUM TIME** 3hrs 30min

ASCENT/GRADIENT 1,247ft (380m) ▲▲▲   **LEVEL OF DIFFICULTY** +++

PATHS Good paths and tracks

LANDSCAPE Open moorland

SUGGESTED MAP OS Explorer OL21 South Pennines

START/FINISH Grid reference: SD936241

DOG FRIENDLINESS Under control as sheep present throughout

PARKING Car parks in centre of Todmorden

PUBLIC TOILETS Brook Street, Todmorden

Todmorden is a border town, standing at the junction of three valley routes. Before the town was included in the old West Riding, the Yorkshire–Lancashire border divided the town in two. Todmorden's splendid town hall, built in an unrestrained classical Greek style, reflects this dual personality. On top of the town hall are carved figures which represent, on one side, the Lancashire cotton trade, and, on the other side, Yorkshire agriculture and engineering.

STOODLEY PIKE

Stoodley Pike is a ubiquitous sight around the Calder Valley, an unmistakable landmark. West Yorkshire is full of monuments built on prominent outcrops, but few of them dominate the view in quite the way that Stoodley Pike does.

In 1814, a trio of patriotic Todmorden men convened in a local pub to discuss the building of a monument to commemorate the end of the Napoleonic War. They organised a public subscription, and raised enough money to erect a monument, 1,476ft (450m) on Langfield Edge, overlooking the town. Construction was halted, briefly, when Napoleon rallied his troops, and was not completed until the following year, when Napoleon was finally defeated at the Battle of Waterloo.

This original monument was undone by the Pennine weather – it collapsed in 1854, on the day that the Crimean War broke out. Another group of locals came together to raise more money. The Stoodley Pike we see today is Mark II: 131ft (40m) high and was built to commemorate the ending of the Crimean War.

As well as being popular with local walkers, the Pike is visited by walkers on the Pennine Way. Remember to pack a torch so that you can climb the unlit stone steps inside the monument to reach a viewing platform with stunning, panoramic views over Calderdale and beyond.

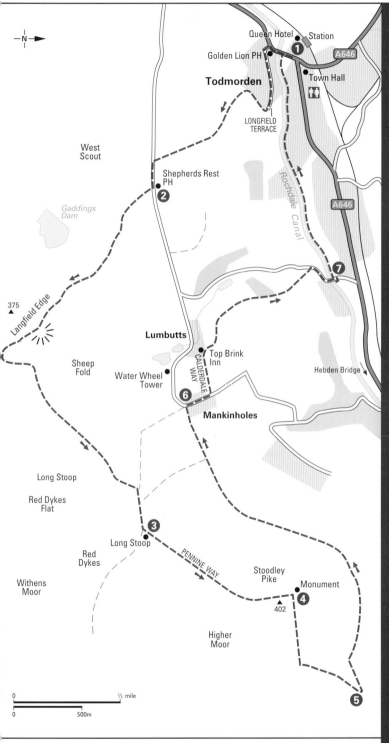

1 From the town hall in the centre of Todmorden, take the Rochdale road (A6033), cross the canal, turning left and immediately left again around the Golden Lion pub (closed due to flooding in 2012) to walk up Longfield Road. Keep ahead as the main street veers away to new houses, but then swing right with Longfield Road up to Longfield Terrace at the end. Just before the row of houses, bear left on a track climbing between the fields behind. When the track forks, keep left to a farm, from where you will get the first glimpse of Stoodley Pike on the horizon ahead. Continue along the farm track to a road. Go left to find the Shepherds Rest pub.

2 Opposite the pub, take a track leading through a gate, uphill, on to Langfield Common. Keep ahead past a waymark along a distinct and well-graded path that rises across the steep hillside below Langfield Edge. Levelling at the top, it is joined by another path to round the head of the clough. The way runs on above the edge, eventually intersecting a broader path, the Pennine Way. Go left towards the distant monument.

3 Passing a stone seat, the path falls to a junction. Climb ahead past the leaning ancient waystone of Long Stoop. The way soon levels for the final stretch to the tower, 0.75 miles (1.2km) further on.

4 From the monument, swing right, walking down to a wall stile. After a few paces cross a second stile in the adjacent wall, from which the path drops more steeply to a lower track, London Road.

5 Follow the track left in a long and gentle descent to come out on to a lane. Go right, into the hamlet of Mankinholes.

6 After 0.25 miles (400m), opposite a cemetery and former Wesleyan Sunday School, turn off left along a walled path, signed the 'Pennine Bridleway'. It winds between fields to the Top Brink Inn at Lumbutts. Turn right between houses and continue at the field-edge along a causeway path. Passing through a squeeze gap into the third field, bear half right across the slope. Keep going beyond a broken wall, the path shortly closing beside a high fence. Meeting a farm track head downhill to emerge by cottages. Follow the lane right, swinging in front of a converted mill to a bridge spanning the Rochdale Canal.

7 Drop right to the tow path and follow the canal back under the bridge into the centre of Todmorden.

WHERE TO EAT AND DRINK The isolated Shepherds Rest pub is near the beginning of this walk, while the Top Brink Inn at Lumbutts is towards the end. Back in town you can try the Queen Hotel by the station.

WHAT TO SEE London Road was a 'cotton famine road'. When the cotton trade suffered one of its periodic slumps, mill owner John Fielden of Todmorden put his men to work on building this road. Fielden also built Dobroyd Castle, now an outdoor activity centre.

Right: A view west on the Pennine Way towards Stoodley Pike, Todmorden (Walk 42)

Hardcastle Crags and Crimsworth Dean

DISTANCE 5 miles (8km)   MINIMUM TIME 2hrs

ASCENT/GRADIENT 935ft (285m) ▲▲▲   LEVEL OF DIFFICULTY ✦✦✦

PATHS Good paths and tracks, plus open pasture, no stiles

LANDSCAPE Woodland, fields and moorland fringe

SUGGESTED MAP OS Explorer OL21 South Pennines

START/FINISH Grid reference: SD987293

DOG FRIENDLINESS Keep on lead near livestock

PARKING National Trust pay-and-display car parks at Midgehole, near Hebden Bridge (accessible via A6033, Keighley Road)

PUBLIC TOILETS At Gibson Mill during opening hours

Hebden Bridge, just 4 miles (6.4km) from the Yorkshire/Lancashire border, has been a popular place to visit ever since the railway was extended across the Pennines, through the Calder Valley. The big attraction was the wooded valley of Hebden Dale – usually called 'Hardcastle Crags' – just a short charabanc ride away. 'Hebden Bridge for Hardcastle Crags' was the stationmaster's cry, as trains approached the station. Here were shady woods, easy riverside walks and places to spread out a picnic blanket. To people who lived in the terraced streets of Bradford, Leeds or Halifax, Hardcastle Crags must have seemed idyllic. The steep-sided valley reminded Swiss visitors of their own country, and became 'Little Switzerland' – at least to the writers of tourist brochures. The only disappointment, in fact, was the crags themselves: unassuming gritstone outcrops, almost hidden by trees.

INDUSTRIAL DEMANDS

The Industrial Revolution created a huge demand for water: for mills, factories and domestic use. To quench the thirst of the rapidly expanding textile towns, many steep-sided valleys, known in the South Pennines as cloughs, were dammed to create reservoirs. Six of these lie within easy walking distance of Hardcastle Crags. They represented huge feats of civil engineering by the hundreds of navvies who built them, around the end of the 19th century, with picks and shovels. The men were housed in a shanty town, known as Dawson City and both men and materials were transported to the work sites by a convoluted steam-powered railway system that crossed the valley on an elaborate wooden viaduct.

Hardcastle Crags has narrowly escaped the indignity of being turned into a reservoir. Three times plans were drawn up to flood the

Left: Hardcastle Crags (Walk 43)

valley. And three times, thankfully, wiser counsels prevailed and the plans were turned down. Lord Savile, a major landowner in the area, once owned the valley. It was he who supplemented the natural woodland with plantings of new trees – particularly pines – and laid out the walks and the carriage drive. In 1948 Lord Savile donated Hardcastle Crags, and the nearby valley of Crimsworth Dean, to the National Trust. Because of this bequeathment, the future of this delightful valley looks secure and local people will be able to continue to enjoy this valuable amenity.

Hardcastle Crags are a haven for wildlife. Birders can look out for pied flycatchers, woodpeckers, jays, sparrowhawks and the ubiquitous dipper – which never strays from the environs of Hebden Water. In spring there are displays of bluebells; in summer the woods are filled with birdsong; the beech woods are a riot of colour as the leaves turn each autumn.

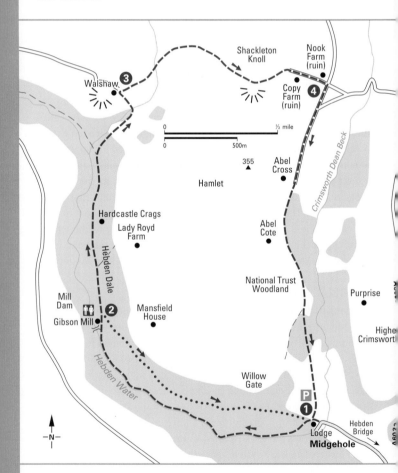

1 From the non-member pay-and-display car park at Midgehole, walk back to the main drive. Go left towards the lodge but, just past the information board, immediately double back right on a path falling to a picnic area beside the river. Keep left whenever there is a choice of paths and continue upstream for a mile (1.6km) to reach Gibson Mill, occasionally climbing above the river where it becomes constricted between rocky banks.

2 Joining the main drive, follow it left beyond the mill, soon passing the crags that give the woods their name. Keep right at a later fork, shortly emerging from the trees and the National Trust estate to join a rough metalled drive. It runs left to the farm and adjacent cottages at Walshaw, which enjoy a terrific prospect along the Hebden Water valley.

3 Just before you reach the houses – when you are opposite some barns – turn sharp right through a gate on to an enclosed track (signed to Crimsworth Dean). Running on as a field track, it peters out beyond another gate to follow a wall over the shoulder of Shackleton Knoll. Approaching the watershed, the path slips through a gate to continue on the wall's opposite flank. Developing as a track, it later turns through another gate and drops into Crimsworth Dean, ending at a junction beside the ruin of Nook Farm. Running the length of the valley, the rough way is the old road from Hebden Bridge to Howarth and is a great walk to contemplate for another day.

4 For now, however, turn right along this elevated track, passing a farm on the left. You can make a short detour right at the next fork to see Abel Cross, actually a pair of old waymarker stones standing beside the track. Return to the main track and continue down the valley, soon re-entering the woodland of the National Trust estate. Keep left at successive forks, eventually returning to the car parks at Midgehole.

WHERE TO EAT AND DRINK The Pack Horse Inn can be found on the unclassified road between Colden and Brierfield, just beyond the wooded valley of Hardcastle Crags. It is one of many solitary, exposed pubs to be found in Pennine Yorkshire, which existed to cater for the drovers and packhorse men of times gone by. The Pack Horse remains a favourite with travellers, but is closed Mondays and lunchtimes other than Sunday between October and Easter.

WHAT TO SEE Hebden Water rushes picturesque through the wooded valley of Hardcastle Crags. These upland rivers and streams are the perfect habitat for an attractive little bird called the dipper. Dark brown, with a blaze of white on the breast, the dipper never strays from water. Unique among British birds, it has perfected the trick of walking underwater.

WHILE YOU'RE THERE Walk the old road from Hebden Bridge to Haworth (it's marked as such on the OS map) that includes the section of track through wooded Crimsworth Dean. The old road is never hard to find, and offers easy walking with terrific views all the way. Have lunch in Haworth, and take the easy way back to Hebden Bridge – by bus.

Hebden Water and Gibson Mill

DISTANCE 2.5 miles (4km)	MINIMUM TIME 1hr

ASCENT/GRADIENT 360ft (110m) ▲▲▲   LEVEL OF DIFFICULTY ✚✚✚

SEE MAP AND INFORMATION PANEL FOR WALK 43

If you only have time to walk to Gibson Mill and back, you will have enjoyed arguably the finest short woodland walk in West Yorkshire. The mill was built 200 years ago, when Hebden Water was harnessed to turn a waterwheel and power the cotton spinning machines. The mill pond, behind the mill itself, was built to maintain a good supply of water, even when the river levels were low. This was not the only mill in the valley, but it's the only one still standing. Gibson Mill itself occupies a romantic setting, deep in the woods, its image beautifully reflected in the adjacent mill pond. But appearances can be deceptive.

The mill was notorious for its poor working conditions. From a report of 1833 we learn that the 22 employees in Gibson Mill were accustomed to a 72-hour week, with children as young as ten starting their working day at 6am and finishing at 7.30pm. Because of their size, the children were able to make repairs to the machines while they were still running. Accidents were common. The children had just two breaks during their day – for breakfast and dinner. It wasn't until 1847 that legislation was passed, to limit the working day for women and children to 'only' ten hours.

The waterwheel stopped turning in 1852, when the mill was converted to steam power. But by the 1890s the mill had become redundant. Due to its attractive situation, however, it was put to a variety of recreational uses. At various times up until World War II, it was a tea room, dance hall, dining saloon, even a roller-skating rink. The mill pond became a rowing lake. An award-winning restoration by the National Trust has since turned it into an excellent, environmentally sustainable 'hands-on' exhibition and visitor centre.

From the non-member pay-and-display car park at Midgehole, walk back to the main drive. Go left and, immediately past the information board, double back right, dropping to a picnic area beside the river. The path continues upstream, occasionally climbing steps over outcrops that overhang the flow and eventually leading to Gibson Mill.

Many good paths and tracks converge here, and all provide excellent walking. But for this short ramble you should join the gravel track (known as the carriage drive) that passes the mill. Walk to the right, still through woodland, as the track leads you back to the car park.

Visiting East Riddlesden Hall

DISTANCE 5 miles (8km)	MINIMUM TIME 2hrs

ASCENT/GRADIENT 623ft (190m) ▲▲▲   LEVEL OF DIFFICULTY ✚✚✚

PATHS Field paths and canal tow path, several stiles

LANDSCAPE Arable landscape and canalside

SUGGESTED MAP OS Explorer 297 Lower Wharfedale

START/FINISH Grid reference: SE098419

DOG FRIENDLINESS Keep on lead near livestock. Dogs not permitted in Hall

PARKING Roadside parking in East Morton

PUBLIC TOILETS East Morton

Now hidden away in the suburbs of Keighley, East Riddlesden Hall is one of West Yorkshire's architectural gems. This gaunt, gritstone manor house is the work of James Murgatroyd, a wealthy yeoman clothier from Halifax. He built it in the 1640s on the site of an even older hall, but of this earlier building only the great hall remains.

Above the battlements of the hall's bothy, James Murgatroyd had two heads carved in stone: a bewigged Charles I and his queen, Henrietta Maria of France accompanied by the legend *Vive le Roy* (long live the king). This was a dangerous time for such strong expressions of allegiance, for the country was divided by civil war and many Royalists were deprived of their possessions for far less. Despite its remoteness from the seats of power in London, the north was quickly drawn into the conflict and many in this part of the country supported the Parliamentarians. Nevertheless, Murgatroyd offered one of his other houses, Hollins at Warley near Halifax, to his king's forces for the storage of weapons. Inevitably it was attacked and fell after a short but fierce battle, in which even the tiles of the roof were ripped off and used as missiles. Although 44 men were taken prisoner, Murgatroyd appears to have got away and managed to complete his building works at East Riddlesden by 1648.

Though surrounded by houses today, East Riddlesden Hall was always a farm. The Augustinian canons from Bolton Priory in nearby Wharfedale dug the pool as a fishpond to provide them with a ready source of food, and it still survives to ornament the front of the hall. There used to be a medieval mill beside the River Aire and, by the hall, the huge 17th-century tithe barn is one of the finest examples in the North of England. It is now used to display a collection of period farm implements.

The hall is remarkable in that it has remained largely unaltered, due to the fact that it was let to tenant farmers during the 18th and 19th centuries. Although the surrounding land was gradually sold off, the hall was bequeathed to the National Trust in 1934 and is one of their must-see properties in the area. Striking features are the rose windows over the entrance porches at the front and back of the hall, which are typical of the 'Halifax' houses found in this part of the South Pennines. Oak-panelled rooms and mullioned windows provide a sympathetic setting for the collections of domestic utensils and Yorkshire oak furniture that date from the 17th and 18th centuries.

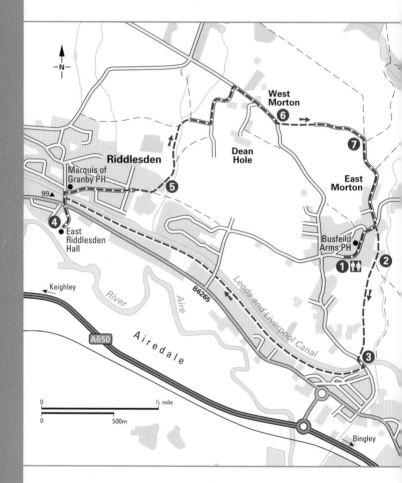

❶ Follow the main road from the toilets past the Busfield Arms. After 150yds (137m) at the crest of the hill, turn right down Little Lane. Go through consecutive gates beside the bottom cottage and continue along a

walled path that leads out to a street, Cliffe Mill Fold.

❷ Swing right and then left into Hawthorne Way, crossing a stile at the end of the cul-de-sac into a field. The path follows the right-hand wall into the next field, but as the wall later curves right, keep ahead to a squeeze gap in the lower boundary. Carry on down through trees and then along a fenced path between paddocks to emerge over a stile onto a road by the Leeds and Liverpool Canal.

3 Cross the swing bridge and follow the tow path to the right for 1.5 miles (2.4km), passing beneath a stone bridge to arrive at the next swing bridge. Leave the canal there and follow the lane left to the B6265, crossing beside the traffic lights to East Riddlesden Hall opposite.

4 Having looked around the hall, retrace your steps to the canal and cross the swing bridge. Immediately turn right in front of the Marquis of Granby pub along Hospital Road. At the end, carry on along a contained path immediately left of the old gates to the former isolation hospital. Skirting a housing development, cross two streets. Some 15yds (14m) beyond the second street, turn off through a gap stile in the left wall.

Follow a paved walkway up through the estate and out between houses at the top to a stile.

5 Cross a small paddock to a second stile and continue at the field-edge beside a beck. Beyond a gate, stick with the ongoing track, which soon swings over a bridge and into a farmyard. Walk on past cottages to meet a bend in a lane. Turn left and follow it to a junction at the top. Go right and walk for 0.25 miles (400m).

6 Just past the cricket green, where the lane bends right, leave through a squeeze gap by a gate on the left. Walk away by the right wall, keeping ahead through a gate into a second field. Over a stile in the next corner, continue to a squeeze gap on the left from which a walled track leads to Moorlands Farm.

7 Skirt the buildings and leave along its access track. Lower down, swing right past a junction and carry on to meet a lane at the bottom. Go right into East Morton, turning right again at the end to return past the pub.

WHERE TO EAT AND DRINK The Busfeild Arms (named after a prominent local family) at the start of the walk in East Morton, offers good food, if eccentric spelling. The Marquis of Granby, just over the canal from East Riddlesden Hall, offers refreshments at the halfway point.

WHAT TO SEE East Riddlesden Hall is blessed with a cast of ghostly characters. The most famous is the Grey Lady, the wife of a previous lord of the manor, seen wandering from room to room.

WHILE YOU'RE THERE As well as visiting the National Trust's East Riddlesden Hall, which forms the theme for this walk, take a little time to explore the neighbouring mill town of Keighley (pronounced 'Keithlee'). There are still some fine Victorian buildings intact which give an indication of the wealth that the textile industry generated. There is also an excellent indoor market.

On the packhorse trail along Salter Rake

DISTANCE 6 miles (9.7km)	MINIMUM TIME 2hrs 30min

ASCENT/GRADIENT 902ft (275m) ▲▲▲   LEVEL OF DIFFICULTY ✦✦✦

PATHS Good paths and tracks throughout

LANDSCAPE Open moorland, reservoirs and canalside

SUGGESTED MAP OS Explorer OL21 South Pennines

START/FINISH Grid reference: SD943204

DOG FRIENDLINESS Keep on lead throughout the walk, especially around sheep

PARKING Lay-by, 300yds (274m) north of Warland Gate End on A6033, by playing field, between Todmorden and Littleborough

PUBLIC TOILETS None on route

Salter Rake is an old packhorse road which was used particularly for transporting salt from the Cheshire salt mines across the Pennines. When these trading routes were first established, the Calder Valley was largely undrained. The teams of packhorse ponies would keep to the drier high ground, only descending into the valleys to cross rivers on the narrow stone bridges that are so typical of the area.

Most of these causeways (or 'causeys') were paved with stones and, more than three centuries later, the stones still fit snugly together. Looking at the way they are deeply dished, the stones have seen heavy use over the years by countless horses' hooves.

FAMILIAR ROCKS

Gritstone rocks and outcrops are familiar features throughout the South Pennines. The Basin Stone, an odd-shaped rock looks – from one viewpoint, at least – like a fishtail. It is a prominent landmark high on Walsden Moor and was one of the many sites used by travelling Methodist preachers when they delivered their open-air sermons, well away from the watchful eyes of the authorities.

RESERVOIRS

Like many of the reservoirs you will encounter in the South Pennines, the one passed on this walk – Warland – was built to supply water for a canal, as was nearby Light Hazzle Reservoir and also White Holme Reservoir. The Rochdale Canal was built to link Manchester to the Calder and Hebble Navigation at Sowerby Bridge. By the 1920s there was very little commercial traffic still using it, so the reservoirs were converted to an alternative use and joined the complex of water supply systems built to slake the thirst of East Lancashire's mill towns.

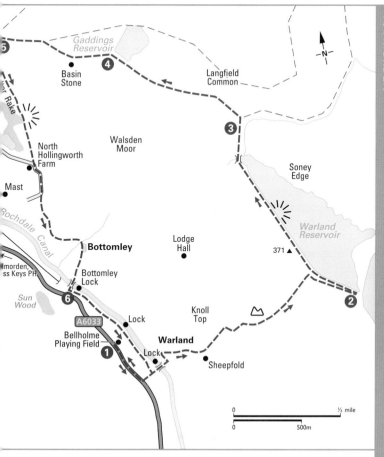

① Walk southeast along the road for 300yds (274m), passing the former Bird i'th Hand pub to take a track on the left past cottages, Warland Gate End. Cross the Rochdale Canal on a swing bridge and follow the track over a stream to zigzag steeply up the hill. Where the track later forks, keep right through an ornamental gate towards Calflee House. Turn right when you reach a T-junction. Approaching the house, go through a second gate and swing left on a track that leads up to another house. Pass around the back of the building to find a field gate and continue across the open moor on a rising rough track. As you approach the retaining embankment of Warland Reservoir, follow the track to the right, which slants upwards to reach the reservoir.

② Double back left along the top of the dam, from which there are terrific views over Calderdale and East Lancashire. Cross a bridge at the northern end of the reservoir, and keep on the track as it follows a drainage channel.

③ When both track and channel wheel to the right, go left in front of a stone bridge, to follow a flagged path in the direction of another, smaller lake, Gaddings Reservoir. It was reputedly built with convict labour and was intended to supplement water supplies for the textile mills in the valley disrupted by the construction of the canal. On the distant skylines ahead and to the right are two of the many windfarms, built to take advantage of the abundant winds that sweep the Pennines.

❹ Bear half left at the far end of the reservoir, down stone steps and continue along a clear path that soon passes close to the curiously-shaped outcrop called the Basin Stone. Shortly you will come to a meeting of paths, marked with a small waymarker post.

❺ Turn left here, on a path that's soon delineated by causeway stones; you are now following Salter Rake, an old packhorse road. Enjoy excellent views over Walsden as you make a gradual descent, still across open moorland, then accompanying a wall. Eventually, leave the moor through

a gate and continue to a junction opposite a mullion-windowed farmhouse. Bear left to pass a second house, Hollingworth Gate, walking through a gate back onto the moor. Immediately branch right off the track on to a causeway path, marked as the Pennine Bridleway. It later swings above another farmhouse and before long, winds across a beck to reach the tiny hillside settlement of Bottomley. Go right here, down a metalled track, but then bear immediately right again, through a gate, along a cobbled, walled path heading directly downhill. This will take you directly to the Rochdale Canal.

❻ Cross the canal by the side of Bottomley Lock, and walk left along the canal tow path. An easy 0.5 mile-long (800m) stroll returns you to the swing bridge straddling the Yorkshire–Lancashire border over which you set out. Go right to the main road and right again back to your car.

WHERE TO EAT AND DRINK A mile (1.6km) down the road towards Todmorden is the Cross Keys, where there is a Mediterranean theme to the menu. Its name came with the opening of Walsden's church dedicated to St Peter – whose symbol is a pair of crossed keys.

WHAT TO SEE Steanor Bottom tollhouse is a small hexagonal building dating from the 1820s. You will find it on the main A6033 road, to the south of Warland Gate End. The tollhouse has been restored and retains its notice board presenting the tariff for all the different kinds of traffic, from sheep to carts.

WHILE YOU'RE THERE Southeast of Walsden, just off the A68 is a short, steep track over the Pennine watershed of Blackstone Edge. This elaborately paved path, about 13ft (4m) wide and with a stone channel down the middle, is marked on the Ordnance Survey map as a Roman road, but opinions about its origins are divided. One thing is sure: if it is Roman, it's one of the best-preserved examples in the country.

Right: Rochdale Canal (Walk 46)

The Bridestone Rocks from Lydgate

DISTANCE 6 miles (9.7km)	MINIMUM TIME 2hrs 45min

ASCENT/GRADIENT 1,296ft (395m) ▲▲▲   LEVEL OF DIFFICULTY ✦✦✦

PATHS Moorland and packhorse paths, some quiet roads

LANDSCAPE Steep-sided valley and open moorland

SUGGESTED MAP OS Explorer OL21 South Pennines

START/FINISH Grid reference: SD923255

DOG FRIENDLINESS Keep on lead along lanes and near grazing sheep

PARKING Roadside parking in Lydgate, 1.5 miles (2.4km) out of Todmorden, on A646, signposted to Burnley

PUBLIC TOILETS None on route

The Long Causeway, between Halifax and Burnley, is an ancient trading route, possibly dating back to the Bronze Age. Crosses and waymarker stones helped to guide travellers across the moorland wastes, though most of them have been lost or damaged in the intervening years. Amazingly, Mount Cross has survived intact: a splendid, though crudely carved, example of the Celtic wheel head design. Opinions differ about its age but it is certainly the oldest man-made artefact in the area, erected at least a thousand years ago.

THE BRIDESTONES

The impressive piles of Orchan Rocks and Whirlaw Rocks are both encountered on this walk. But the most intriguing rock formations are to be found at the Bridestones. One rock has been weathered by wind and water into a teardrop shape, and stands on a base that looks far too slender to support its great weight. It resembles a rock in the North York Moors National Park, which is also known as the Bridestone.

WIND POWER

Further along the edge to the northwest are the tall turbines of Coal Clough Windfarm. With a capacity of around 9.6 megawatts, enough to power around 5,500 homes, it was opened in 1992 and was one of the first such schemes to be commissioned in the UK. It is now (2013) reaching the end of its life and it is planned to replace the 24 turbines with eight bigger structures, capable of producing 16 megawatts.

CLIVIGER VALLEY

The Cliviger Valley links two towns – Todmorden in West Yorkshire and Burnley in Lancashire – that expanded with the textile trade, and then suffered when that trade went into decline. The valley itself is narrow and steep-sided, in places almost a gorge. Into the cramped confines of the valley are shoehorned the road, railway line, the infant River Calder and communities such as Portsmouth, Cornholme and Lydgate that grew up around the textile mills. The mills were powered by fast-flowing becks, running off the steep hillsides. The valley is almost a microcosm of the Industrial Revolution: by no means beautiful, but full of character. This area is particularly well provided with good footpaths, some of them still paved with their original causeway stones.

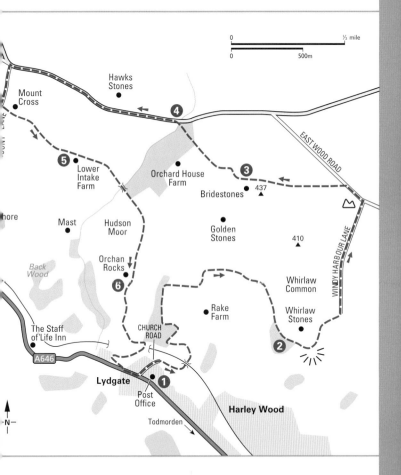

❶ From the post office in Lydgate, take Church Road. At the end go right into Owlers Walk and continue along a contained path. Meeting a track at its end, follow it beneath a railway bridge and up to Stannally Farm. Walk past the buildings and swing right as the track zigzags steeply up the wooded hillside. Eventually breaking out onto the edge of open moor it swings right towards a farm. Pass left of the farmhouse and then bear left up a narrower walled track. When you meet another walled track, go right towards a rocky outcrop on the first horizon. Beyond two gates, the path crosses onto the rough common that aprons Whirlaw Stones.

② A causeway path skirts the base of the outcrop giving panoramic views of the Cliviger Valley, Todmorden and Stoodley Pike. Keep going through gates until you reach a junction above East Whirlaw Farm. There turn sharp left along a stony track that winds up beside the outcrop to meet the end of Windy Harbour Lane. Carry on up the lane, which shortly leads to Eastwood Road. Go left for just 150yds (137m). Where the wall ends, take a kissing gate on the left. A grassy path leads you to another fascinating collection of rocks, known as the Bridestones.

③ Continue past the Bridestones across a landscape of scattered boulders. Keep ahead beyond the trig point, dropping to cross a ruined wall. Keep ahead past wayposts, the path curving above the edge and eventually falling to a gate and stile. Follow a track right out to a lane.

④ Go left, along the road for 0.75 miles (1.2km), passing below the Hawks Stones on the right and a handful of houses, until you come to a minor road on the left. This is Mount Lane, signed to Shore. Walk down for 300yds (274m) before turning left on to a broad bridleway. Look out for Mount Cross, which stands a short way along, over the wall in a field to your left.

⑤ Bear left past Lower Intake Farm on a path that soon resumes as a track. Cross an intersecting track and, later, a bridge spanning a stream before reaching a stile, 250yds (229m) further along on the right. Ignore the stile, but take the adjacent track, which drops alongside a wall past another gritstone outcrop known as Orchan Rocks.

⑥ Where the wall bears left, beyond the rocks, follow it downhill to a stile. You now join a farm track that makes a serpentine descent through woodland back to Lydgate. Reaching the former Board School, now the Robin Wood Activity Centre, turn sharp left back to the main road.

WHERE TO EAT AND DRINK The Staff of Life, on the main A646 at Lydgate, is a cosy 'real ale' pub offering a warm welcome and home-made food, using fresh, organic and locally sourced produce.

WHAT TO SEE In geological terms, the South Pennines are largely made up of Millstone grit and coarse sandstone. Where the gritstone is visible, it forms rocky crags and outcrops, like those encountered on this walk. The typical landscape is moorland of heather and peat, driven by steep-sided valleys. Here, in the cramped confines of the deep Cliviger Valley, road, rail and river cross and re-cross each other many times over.

WHILE YOU'RE THERE If you continue along the Long Causeway, you'll soon come to Coal Clough Windfarm. These huge wind turbines can be found on the crest of many South Pennine hills, attracting strong winds and equally strong opinions. To some people they represent a sustainable future for energy, to others they are ugly intrusions on the landscape.

Jumble Hole and Colden Clough

DISTANCE 6 miles (9.7km)	MINIMUM TIME 2hrs 30min

ASCENT/GRADIENT 1,132ft (345m) ▲▲▲   LEVEL OF DIFFICULTY ✛✛✛

PATHS Good paths, many stiles

LANDSCAPE Steep-sided valleys, fields and woodland

SUGGESTED MAP OS Explorer OL21 South Pennines

START/FINISH Grid reference: SD991271

DOG FRIENDLINESS Keep on lead near livestock and roads

PARKING Pay-and-display car parks in Hebden Bridge

PUBLIC TOILETS Hebden Bridge and Heptonstall

This walk links the little town of Hebden Bridge with the old hand-weaving village of Heptonstall, using sections of the Calderdale Way. The hill village of Heptonstall is by far the older settlement and was once an important centre of the textile trade. A cursory look at a map shows Heptonstall to be at the hub of a complex network of old trackways, mostly used by packhorse trains carrying wool and cotton. Heptonstall's Cloth Hall dates back to the 16th century, when Hebden Bridge was little more than a river crossing on a packhorse causeway.

WHEELS OF INDUSTRY

Heptonstall prospered when textiles were still a cottage industry, with spinning and weaving being undertaken in isolated farmhouses. As the processes became mechanised during the Industrial Revolution, communities sprang up wherever a ready supply of running water could turn waterwheels to drive the new machinery. Heptonstall was literally left high and dry and a new settlement grew down in the valley at the confluence of two fast-flowing rivers, the Calder and Hebden Water. There, large mills enabled the textile processes to be developed on a truly industrial scale.

At one time more than 30 mills in Hebden Bridge belched thick smoke into the Calder Valley, the fug only lifting during Wakes Week, the mill-hands' traditional holiday. With Hebden Bridge being hemmed in by hills, and the mills occupying much of the available land on the valley bottom, the workers' houses had to be built up the steep slopes, hence the 'top and bottom' houses, one dwelling on top of another.

Few looms clatter today and Hebden Bridge has reinvented itself as the 'capital' of Upper Calderdale. The town is known for it's excellent walking country, Bohemian population, narrowboat trips along the Rochdale Canal and its very popular summer arts festival.

Jumble Hole Clough is a typical South Pennine steep-sided, wooded valley. Though a tranquil scene today, this little valley was once a centre of industry, with four mills exploiting the fast-flowing beck as it made its way down to join the River Calder. You can see remains of all these mills, and some of their mill ponds, on this walk; but the most intriguing relic is Staups Mill, now an evocative ruin, near the top of Jumble Hole Clough.

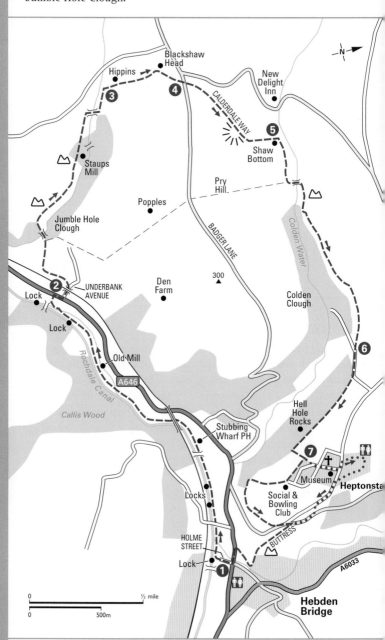

1 Begin along Holme Street, off the main A646 just east of the bridge, to the Rochdale Canal. Go right to follow the tow path beneath two bridges, past the Stubbing Wharf pub and beneath a railway bridge. Carry on for another 0.75 miles (1.2km) before turning off before the next bridge to follow a track to reach the A646.

2 Cross the road and turn right for 75yds (69m) to take Underbank Avenue, on the left. Go under the railway and then left again, past houses (here another road comes through the viaduct). Go sharp right on a track past a mill, and follow the beck up into the woodland of Jumble Hole Clough. Where the track later swings sharp right, leave across a stone bridge on to a track rising steeply through a hairpin. Higher up as it wheels left, take the narrow path ahead to continue above the beck. Ignore a later intersecting path and climb beyond to a stile. Join another path down to Staups Mill. The climb resumes beside the ruin to reach a footbridge. Scale the opposite bank and go left in front of a signpost by a gap in a wall to come out at Hippins.

3 Join the Calderdale Way, turning right up a track between farm buildings to a stile. Follow a path to the next stile and on beside a wall. Cross a track at Apple Tree Farm and continue over a couple of stiles on a causeway to a row of cottages. Pass the end of the terrace, crossing more stiles and a rough pasture to a kissing gate. Follow the onward causeway to a farm, there following a track out to the lane at Blackshaw Head.

4 Cross to a small gate almost opposite and bear half right across the field to a stile, then follow the right edge of the next field. Continue on a diagonal line across successive fields, eventually reaching a walled track. Walk down to Shaw Bottom and bear left beside the house to a junction.

5 The New Delight Inn is left, but the route lies to the right, the way degrading to a stony track. After 200yds (183m), bear left beside a waypost on a stepped path dropping steeply to cross Colden Water. Take the rising path, but then keep right higher up to follow a stone causeway along the valley side above the trees. Carry on as you later break out into a field. Over a stile at the far corner, ignore the adjacent gate and swing around the wall corner to pick up the continuing flagged path. Eventually meeting a rising track, go left to a junction and turn right on a tarmac drive. Bear off left behind a cottage, the causeway resuming over a stile beyond. Shortly at an intersecting track, go right and follow it to a lane.

6 Walk up the hill, leaving just before a bend through a gap in the right-hand wall. From here your path goes through woodland. Emerging from the trees, continue above the edge to Hell Hole Rocks. Turn away from the viewpoint along a walled path between house gardens. Cross a street to the ongoing path, which shortly meets a track behind houses.

7 Go right, emerging opposite the Social and Bowling Club. Turn right on a contained path. As the ground falls away, curve left by the boundary, eventually dropping through a wall onto a crossing path. Walk left to meet a track and go right to a junction. Bear left along the lower, main road, doubling sharply right after 50yds (46m) onto the Buttress, an old packhorse trail that drops steeply back to Hebden Bridge.

On and up to Heptonstall

DISTANCE 6.5 miles (10.4km)   MINIMUM TIME 3hrs 30min

ASCENT/GRADIENT 1,164ft (355m) ▲▲▲   LEVEL OF DIFFICULTY ✚✚✚

SEE MAP AND INFORMATION PANEL FOR WALK 48

If you extend Walk 48 with a look around Heptonstall, you won't be disappointed. It's a gem. Allow an hour or more to explore and soak up its unique atmosphere.

Turning left at Point **7**, cross a street to enter the old village by the church. The gritstone houses huddle closely together, as though sheltering from the prevailing wind; the effect is captivating. The old heart of Heptonstall is now a conservation area: a splendid example of a pre-industrial hill village. While Haworth sold its soul to the tourist trade, Heptonstall remains handsomely authentic.

The old parish churchyard is paved with gravestones. It is shared, almost uniquely, by two churches: a capacious Victorian edifice and the ruins of the old medieval church. This is the resting place of David Hartley, King of the Coiners, who was hanged in 1779 for his part in the illegal 'clipping' of gold coins. In the new graveyard nearby, the grave of

Sylvia Plath has become a shrine for lovers of her brittle, brilliant poetry.

The Old Grammar School by the medieval church is now a museum and the Old Cloth Hall still stands on the cobbled main street. In Weavers Square, every Good Friday, the Pace Egg Play is performed by local players. It is a rumbustious tale of good against evil, its origins lost in time.

The Methodist Chapel off Northgate claims to be the country's oldest in continuous use and dates back to 1764. It was built to specifications laid down by John Wesley himself, who preached here on a number of occasions. He chose the octagonal shape because it offered 'no corner in which the devil can hide'.

Follow the cobbled main street downhill for 300yds (274m). Take the second footpath signed off left, descending flights of steps to a lower road. Go right and then branch left down a steep packhorse road, the Buttress, back into Hebden Bridge.

WHERE TO EAT AND DRINK New Delight Inn is conveniently situated at the halfway point of the walk. Serving local beers and imaginative food, it is the ideal spot for lunch. And, if the urge to continue walking deserts you, you can pick up a little country bus outside the door that will take you back to Hebden Bridge via the cobbled street of Heptonstall.

The broadleaved woodlands of Harden Beck

DISTANCE 2.5 miles (4km)	MINIMUM TIME 1hr

ASCENT/GRADIENT 246ft (75m) ▲▲▲   LEVEL OF DIFFICULTY ✚✚✚

PATHS Woodland paths and tracks, field paths

LANDSCAPE Deciduous woodland and arable land

SUGGESTED MAP OS Explorer 288 Bradford & Huddersfield, and Explorer OL21 South Pennines

START/FINISH Grid reference: SE088378

DOG FRIENDLINESS Dogs can be off lead in woodland

PARKING From Harden, take Wilsden Road to roadside parking at bottom of hill, just before bridge and The Malt Shovel Inn

PUBLIC TOILETS None on route

A FORGOTTEN PAST

Today, the unassuming valley enclosing Harden Beck and Goit Stock Woods is a quiet, little visited backwater. But it wasn't always the case for, by the beginning of the 19th century, there were at least three textile mills processing silk, cotton and worsteds crowded within its narrow confines and using the fast-flowing stream to power the spinning and weaving machines. The buildings of two have survived: Harden Bridge, which is now used by light industry and Bents Mill at Hallas Bridge, which has been converted for housing. The terraced cottages, built nearby to house the mill workers, are still lived in.

A TOURIST RESORT

But times change, and by the beginning of the 20th century, despite being converted to steam, the relative isolation of Goit Stock Mill left it uneconomic. By then, however, the inherent beauty of the valley, its woods and a modestly spectacular waterfall began to draw visitors, eager for a day away from their workaday lives in the big mills of the surrounding towns. With railways serving both Bingley and Cullingworth, the 'Happy Valley' soon became popular and part of Goit Stock Mill was converted to a ballroom and cafe. Crowds flocked to this spot and reports say that the 1927 May Bank Holiday drew 20,000 people. Sadly it turned out to be a tragic day, for that evening a fire destroyed the dance floor and the instruments of the Wilsden Brass Band, who were providing the entertainment. All that remains today is the chimney of the old steam engine on the hillside.

A QUIET SANCTUARY

Cloaked in deciduous woodland, the valley has become a haven for wildlife, supporting birds such as jays, tree creepers, woodpeckers and many small songbirds that build their nests amongst the trees and bushes. You might even see a dipper probing the pebbles of the sparkling beck for insects.

The falls themselves were created by the differential erosion of a band of soft shale underlying the gritstone rock, which, as it is worn away, eventually causes the hard rock to collapse, leaving the overhanging lip of the fall.

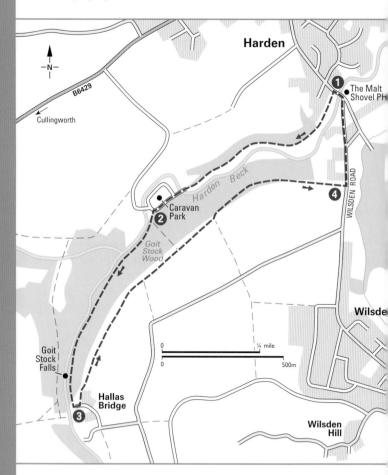

1 From the parking area, walk downhill to take, just before the bridge, the second turning off on the right into Goit Stock Lane. Beyond a terrace of cottages, built to house the workers at Harden Beck Mill, the ongoing rough lane crosses a

cattlegrid and afterward soon joins the stream along the base of the valley below Crag Wood. The track later crosses a bridge to run between a residential caravan park and its parking spaces. The Goit Stock Mill lay towards the top end of this residential caravan site, its impressive, tall chimney still standing.

② At the far end, keep ahead to pass Calgary Lodge and enter Goit Stock Wood. Ignore the path off left and walk forward above Harden Beck along the Millennium Way for some 0.25 miles (400m) to reach the first and largest of the two waterfalls. The continuing path clambers up the rocks beside the fall; and although a handrail has been installed, care is required as the rocks can be slippery. Carry on past a second, smaller cascade and cross a plank bridge, soon emerging onto a crossing bridlepath above Hallas Bridge by the third of the valley's mills built in this short stretch of valley.

③ Turn left up the hill, going left again in front of a terrace of stone cottages. At the end of the street, climb steps to a stile and walk on at the left edge of successive pastures above the wood. At the far end of the fifth field, the path slips through a gap stile to continue within the upper fringe of the wood. Soon joined by another path from the left, keep going across another stile to then leave the trees behind. Follow the field-edge past another row of cottages to emerge over a final stile and onto Wilsden Road.

④ Go left past a garden centre, where there is a cafe. As the road then bends right, keep ahead down a steep, narrow lane, Mill Hill Top. Rejoining the main road at the bottom, walk left past The Malt Shovel Inn to the parking area.

WHERE TO EAT AND DRINK The Malt Shovel Inn is a handsome 16th-century pub with mullioned windows, close by the bridge over Harden Beck. There's a good selection of bar meals on offer; if the weather is kind you can eat on the patio or in the large, beckside beer garden.

WHAT TO SEE Much of West Yorkshire is uncompromisingly urban, but one unexpected pleasure is to find so much broadleaved woodland here. In more celebrated landscapes (the Lake District and North York Moors), too much ancient woodland has been supplanted by the serried ranks of conifer trees, which offer little to walkers or wildlife. Goit Stock is one of many delightful and deciduous woods that make welcome green oases in the metropolitan county, supporting a great variety of animals, birds and plants.

WHILE YOU'RE THERE The little stone village of Harden abuts on to the Bingley St Ives Estate. This short walk through Goit Stock Wood would make an ideal morning stroll, with lunch at the Malt Shovel nearby, followed by a leisurely exploration of the wooded hillside of St Ives. You may also like to explore the group of villages which occupy the high land between Bradford, Bingley and Keighley. Wilsden faces Harden across Harden Beck, Cullingworth lies higher up the valley. A delightful network of old lanes link up with Denholme and the historic conservation village of Thornton where the Brontë children were born. There is a Village Trail around Thornton's cobbled streets, centred on the Brontës' birthplace.

Overleaf: Goit Stock Falls in the heart of Goit Stock Wood, Harden (Walk 50)